THE *P* IS SILENT

Preach

LISA G. SAUNDERS

United Writers Press
Asheville, N.C.
2022

ISBN: 978-1-952248-24-5

Published in conjunction with
United Writers Press
Asheville, N.C.
www.UnitedWritersPress.com

Cover and interior design by Steve Mead.

Printed in the U.S.A.

For Caroline, Julia Gray and Rob

Contents

Chapter 1

The P Is Silent

I dare you.

I dare you not only to keep my attention, but to prove worthy of it.

I dare you to enlighten, comfort, or rouse me. I dare you to say anything relevant to my weights and worries. I dare you to help me breathe, hope, change, forgive, or love. I. Dare. You.

I am a preacher, and every time I preach, I feel that gauntlet thrown down before me. My goal is to give listeners a sermon that holds their attention, connects to their concerns, cracks open scripture to reveal something alive and feathered within, and goes down like a cup of cool water for the parched and a cup of joe for the dispirited. I aim for a message that jibes with the way that Jesus lived, that disturbs without dissing, that makes us see God in our corner, and ourselves through God's eyes—and when I am finished, leaves my listeners coming close to wishing that I weren't.

In other, and fewer words, the "p" in *preach* has to be silent. I need to reach people.

I am a priest in the Episcopal Church. Episcopalians are self-deprecating enough to call ourselves "God's frozen chosen." No one shouts "Amen!" while I preach. I know I am successful in the pulpit when the congregation *is* frozen. When no one fidgets. It is encouraging when I see the brain surgeon listening, but when a child who brought a Harry Potter book to read during the sermon looks up, I know I hit pay dirt.

1

Birdwatchers keep one eye on the sky, and I keep an ear out for what preaches. My husband jokes that he and our children are just sermon fodder. Friends claim they have to be careful around me or they might wind up in a Sunday morning sermon and many have. They don't have to do or say something especially profound or heroic. I mine for and find gold in everyday situations.

In seminary, Milton Crum, my professor for homiletics (a fancy word for preaching), asked whether we could change someone's life with a sermon. My first reaction was to think that was silly. Over the top. Of course not! Next Dr. Crum asked, "Then why are you preaching?"

Yikes. I hadn't thought of it that way.

I am not a child of the Sixties. I was, however, a child *during* the Sixties. By the third grade I was familiar with the adjective "psychedelic." My homework assignment was to write a paragraph using at least five of the week's spelling words. I threw in "sychedelic" to impress my teacher. My mom proofread the paragraph. "You misspelled 'psychedelic,' she said.

I was flabbergasted to learn that the word started with a "p."

"It comes from the Greek language," my mother said, but before she could continue her etymology lesson, my dad chimed in.

"The "p" is silent," he announced. "Like the "p" in *swimming.*"

Mom shot Dad a look. I had seen her give him that look before. It said both *mad at you* and *not mad at you* at the same time. I was missing something.

"But there's no "p" in *swimming!*" I countered.

Dad just smiled.

Thirty minutes later I came back to him, laughing, repeating the punchline: "Like the pee! In swimming!"

I was not only proud that Dad's joke hadn't gone over my head, I was giddy with how words enabled me to see two things at once. I saw something familiar in a new way. It delighted me. What other surprising revelations were hiding out there in the world?

Jesus compared the kingdom of God to a treasure hidden in a field, one that when found is worth selling all you own to buy the field. A good sermon can be like walking in that field. Listeners pocket something useful, helpful, or insightful. Sometimes a good sermon puts an annoying rock in your shoe you can't ignore. In a great sermon, listeners discover that *they* are the hidden treasure.

Professor Crum insisted that his seminary students learn his method of preaching. A manuscript or note cards were taboo. Crum said our purpose was to create a moment of *metanoia*. It was a method that felt vaguely psychedelic. *Metanoia* is a Greek word meaning "a change of heart or mind." To learn the Crum method of preaching, we presented first the tired, conventional way of seeing life, and then in a flash, yanked the curtain back and revealed the upside down, counter-cultural good news of the gospel.

Though fewer folks go to church and listen to sermons than when I stared preaching, people are not becoming less religious. As David Zahl writes in *Seculosity*, people are just as religious as they ever were, but now they are religious about politics, careers, romance, food, parenting, fitness, and technology.[1] I contend that part of the popularity of podcasts is their sermonic quality, offering hope, encouragement, entertainment, advice, relevance, context, and good stories.

---

[1]   *Seculosity: How Career, Parenting, Technology, Food, Politics, and Romance Became Our New Religion and What to Do about It* by David Zahl, copyright 2019.

People crave community as much as they ever did. On Sunday mornings soccer fields are crowded, cycle classes sold out, and tailgate parties in full swing. New Yorkers drag themselves out of bed, dress up, and when fifty years ago they would have headed to the 11:00 A.M. church service, now they keep their 11:00 A.M. reservation for brunch with friends.

Much of what a church provides can be found in secular rituals that restore, refresh, and reunite people. Alcoholics Anonymous is far better at offering grace and promoting spiritual growth than most religious institutions. Many churches have earned a reputation for dispensing shame and anxiety more than the bread and wine of communion, and hammering fear and guilt in, as my dad used to say, a "back asswards" attempt to sustain membership. Jesus and the church suffer from damaging public relations and weak representation.

But there is danger in throwing the baby out with the bath water. And I am talking about the baby Jesus.

Jesus is described as the cornerstone in scripture, and I believe that his way, his truth, his life *is* rock solid. I also believe that Christ can be found in all things everywhere, but it is in the person Jesus of Nazareth that we are given the clearest and most complex revelation of who God is and who we have the capacity to be.

Using scripture, my sermons, devotions and life experiences as fodder, what follows is how Jesus's life has reached my own. Whether you're familiar with or fuzzy on Jesus's story, I hope you discover something new or something old in a new way. Perhaps my time in the pulpit changes lives for the better and *metanoia* happens. But I know that is only possible when the "p" in *preach* is silent.

PERICOPE (2021)

(A pericope is a selection from a broader body of writing. It is pronounced pah-RICK-o-pee. The p's are not silent.)

I learned a new word: apricity.

Apricity is defined as "the warmth of the sun in winter."

Even its spelling melts a frost. Part April. Part felicity.

A quick internet search revealed that *apricity* is also the name of an Alaskan adventure company, a literary journal, a substance abuse rehab center, a blanket manufacturer, and a Scottish singer.

Apricity is a saving grace in the midst of a pandemic: moments of sun and warmth despite a bracing chill covering our country. I love when I can zip up a jacket and bask in the full sun without getting hot. I am warm while breathing in crisp, cool air. I did not realize that I was apricating.

It is hard to beat the real sun, but virtual apricity has just as cozy an effect. As the saying goes, "One kind word can warm three winter months."

There are multiple ways that we can counter the cold and shine a sunny light on one another. And the best part is when we provide virtual apricity to someone else, it automatically warms us up too. That's why we wind up loving ourselves when we love our neighbors. Smart engineering on God's part.

My computer spellcheck is unfamiliar with apricity. Is it snooty to toss the word into casual conversation? I may apricate and get back to you on that.

CHAPTER 2

CHRISTMAS COCOA

ON CHRISTMAS DAY, people want a sermon that goes down like a cup of warm cocoa. With marshmallows.

Cocoa also goes with Christmas carols, which I sing with gusto. I grew up knowing more about Jesus's birth from singing carols than from reading the bible. The donkey, the innkeeper, the stable, a baby who "no crying he makes" all come from carols, and none are mentioned in the bible. Christmas carols also planted an image in my head of Bethlehem as a sleepy, quaint village aglow under the stars.

Phillips Brooks, an Episcopal priest who preached at Lincoln's funeral, wrote the words to the famous carol "O Little Town of Bethlehem." He visited the Holy Land in the fall of 1865 and journaled about his experience there:

> It was only about two hours on horseback from Jerusalem when we came to Bethlehem, situated on an eastern ridge of a range of hills, surrounded by its terraced gardens … Before dark, we rode out of town to the field where they say the shepherds saw the star. It is a fenced piece of ground with a cave in it, in which, strangely enough, they put the shepherds. Somewhere in those fields we rode through, the shepherds must have been.[2]

On a trip to Israel, I made the same trip as Brooks except not on horseback. I went into the same shepherd's cave. Our group sat down inside and sang "The First Noel." It was sweet and peaceful, and my

---

2   *Letters of Travel* by Phillips Brooks, pages 69-70.

favorite part of the visit to Jesus's birthplace. I loved the journey to Israel, but the city of Bethlehem disappointed. It was nothing like the charmed Bethlehem of snow globes I had grown to love.

Though still on a sloping hill with terraced fields, Bethlehem is not quaint anymore.

Bethlehem is a Palestinian-controlled city, 98% Muslim and 2% Christian. The Israeli government built a wall around Bethlehem in 2003 because too many suicide bombers were believed to come from there. At military checkpoints, everyone entering or leaving the city is stopped. A sign at the checkpoints states that Israelis (more specifically, Jews) are forbidden to enter Bethlehem. The city that had no room in the inn for the Jewish holy family now has no room for any Jew.

The government's wall brought trade in and out of Bethlehem to a grinding halt. Businesses closed. Families are separated. Garbage collection is compromised. Bethlehem now is dirty. Abandoned cars sit on blocks. The amount of trash in the streets is unsettling. Tourism is the city's number one industry, and gift shops and hawkers with wares abound. The site of Jesus's birth is heavily commercialized.

The Church of the Nativity, in what is called Manger Square, is a fortress-like basilica and one of the oldest continuously operating churches in the world, having survived invasions, regime changes, fires, earthquakes, and a siege in 2002, when armed Palestinians hid in the church from Israeli forces for weeks.

The church was built around 330 by Constantine, then nearly destroyed and rebuilt by a Byzantine ruler in a bigger, grander fashion. It is stuffed with icons and candles and gaudy chandeliers. A recent restoration revealed bright, colorful frescoes completely hidden by centuries of candle smoke caked on the walls. A narrow stone staircase leads to a small underground grotto. Tourists funnel through in a slow parade.

Inside the grotto is a heavily draped altar and underneath it lamps hang above a fourteen-point star on the marble floor. The points represent the fourteen generations between King David and Jesus. Tourists are encouraged to kneel down, reach underneath the altar and lay their hand on the star to touch the exact place where Jesus was born.

Yeah, right.

I was too cynical to bother. I was far more touched when our group huddled in a corner of the small grotto, read aloud the story of Jesus's birth from the gospel of Luke and sang "Silent Night" *a capella*.

The holy family struggled to find a place to stay for the night in Bethlehem. Our guide wondered aloud if Mary and Joseph could find no room because Mary's pregnancy was shrouded in scandal. The couple's first Christmas happened far from home in a city of strangers—or worse, near people who knew them well but turned them away.

It makes no difference to me whether Mary was a virgin or not. That is not relevant. (The Roman Catholic doctrine of the Immaculate Conception is not about Jesus's birth. The doctrine asserts that *Mary* was also conceived miraculously, making her entire life untouched by sexual contact.) If the Bethlehem story is a myth, I am okay with that too. Myths convey truths. The bible's story of Jesus's birth emphasizes Jesus's humility and solidarity with the outcast and unwelcome, and that both the poor (shepherds) and the powerful (sages from the east) adored him.

As we pulled out of Bethlehem through another checkpoint, I realized that romanticizing Jesus's birthplace blurred the message that the incarnation took place in a coarse and crude location. God did not take the easy route. Ironically, the entire city of Bethlehem has become a stable.

On Christmas Eve in 1979, an American medical student arrived in Nottingham, England, to begin six weeks of training in obstetrics. A week later he delivered the first baby of the New Year. He was the only occupant at the hospital dormitory; everyone else had gone home for Christmas. The town pubs, restaurants, stores, and banks were closed. Even if a restaurant had been open, he didn't have enough pounds in his wallet to pay for a meal. He spent Christmas Eve alone.

The next day he went to the hospital cafeteria to eat his Christmas dinner, alone. Later in the day, someone knocked on his dormitory door. There was a telephone call for him at the hospital. For him? Who could be calling? His parents were both dead and he had no siblings. And how did anyone know what number to call? How did the man who answered the phone even know where to look for him? It must be someone from hospital administration calling with his orders for the next day. He went to the hospital hoping whoever it was would still be on the line.

Hello?

It was a girl from back home calling long distance! He lit up like a Christmas tree. He was so happy to hear from her, and she was so happy to finally speak to him. They hadn't talked since he left home six weeks earlier. After they hung up, he thought to himself, *I should marry that girl.*

That lonely medical student is now my husband of forty years, and I was the girl on the phone. I suppose he still might have married me if I hadn't tracked him down that Christmas Day, but there is something about Christmas that exposes our longings. This likely comes from being asked since a child: what do you want for Christmas? The season makes us more aware of what we want and what we have—or, sometimes painfully, what we don't have. Christmas comes with the iconic image of a child standing with utter delight before a tree skirted with gifts yet to be unwrapped, and as we age, we don't want so much the gifts as we want the delight.

We want the kind of moment when we feel something loving and lovely open up inside ourselves, something generous and gracious shift within us. In other words, we want to experience hope. Christmas is a time of hope, but not just any kind of hope. The hope of Christmas is not a hope born of rationality or convention. It does not answer to our beck and call. It comes unbidden, unexpectedly, undeservedly and opens our eyes and hearts to seeing and believing things in a new light. It is a hope that understands reindeer that fly and stockings that fill up overnight. It costs nothing and comes to rich and poor alike. It is a hope that helps us trust that *what is* is not *all* there is. It is a hope that was born as it was in Bethlehem, in the unlikeliest circumstances and to ordinary people.

It is best described in my favorite carol, "O Holy Night." It begins with "O holy night, the stars are brightly shining" and then goes on, "A thrill of hope, the weary world rejoices, for yonder breaks a new and glorious morn." Yes, that's it. A thrill of hope. That is the kind of hope we long for at Christmas—a hope that doesn't just pat us on the head, but a hope that makes our eyes shine and our hearts take flight.

Jo and David Clark's only daughter, Sally, was killed by a drunk driver when she was just 19. After Sally's death, her father's pain was evident on his face, in his shoulders. David bore his grief like a shroud of stone.

About six months after her death, David came to see me. I told him that I hoped that one day he would be blessed with a granddaughter. David remembered my words when his son got married, and then again when his daughter-in-law became pregnant. And when a little girl was born to them, that child unlocked something long missing in David.

David wrote a book, and at a busy book-signing, his three-year-old granddaughter broke free from the crowd, ran up to him, and leapt into his arms. As she laid her head on his shoulder, that was when I saw it. There. On David's beaming face. The thrill of hope.

That's why we go to all the romanticizing trouble at Christmas—the shopping, decorating, baking, traveling, gift giving—the promise that the child of Bethlehem might unlock something missing in us, that we might experience the thrill of hope, that we might know God came to earth at Christmas to reveal his delight in us. The older I become, the more I realize that the thrill comes just as surely, perhaps even more completely and divinely, not only when I am given hope, but when I can offer hope to another.

I was a skeptic in Bethlehem when it came to laying my hand on the supposed place where Jesus was born. Then I realized that I *can* put my hand on the exact place of Christ's birth. Anyone can. We can take our hand and place it over our heart. Here. Here is the place of Jesus's birth that matters most.

Perhaps that is more cheese than cocoa.

For me, Bethlehem's significance surpasses that of Calvary's because it reveals God's choice to be near us in our messy, grime-caked lives. It is the wonder of all wonders that here, in us and with us, is where God is born and still lives.

Phillip Brooks must have felt this too, for the last stanza of his famous carol "O Little Town of Bethlehem" sings out the same:

O holy child of Bethlehem descend to us, we pray, cast out our sin and enter in, be born in us today. We hear the Christmas angels the great glad tidings tell, O come to us, abide with us, our Lord Emmanuel.

PERICOPE (2015)

Just before Christmas I visited Marian, who lives at a memory care facility. I found her in a noisy common living area. After we chatted for a while, I asked if she wanted to share communion with me. She said yes, and I pushed her wheelchair toward her room, where we could have some quiet and privacy. We rolled past a man who was also in a wheelchair. Marian looked back at me. "Can we invite him to join us?" I was happy to oblige, but pretty certain we would be turned down.

"Excuse me, sir, would you care to join the two of us and have communion?"

"What a blessing that would be," the man said brightly. "I would enjoy that."

"Great!" I said. "My name is Lisa. What's yours?"

"I'm Bernie. There's a table at the end of the hallway we can use. There's only one chair, but she and I already have our chairs."

Bernie "walked" his wheelchair *à* la Fred Flintstone down the hall. "Is that real wine in there?" he asked as he watched me pour communion wine into the small chalice. "I've never touched a drop of wine my whole life."

"Well, we don't want to change that today!" I said.

Another resident came out of her room and walked her wheelchair in the same fashion as Bernie had over to our small circle. I asked her name. No response.

"Do you know her?" I asked.

Bernie looked back at the woman, and then turned to me. "I've seen her before," he said.

I asked the woman if she wanted communion. She nodded yes. We began with three of the four of us heartily singing "O Little Town of Bethlehem." I prayed, thanking God for community and communion. We said the Lord's Prayer and shared communion. Bernie waved his wafer in the chalice, just shy of touching the wine. The woman who joined us last tipped the cup back and finished it. Then she backed her wheelchair out of our circle and headed to her room.

"Well," Bernie said, "we just lost a third of our congregation."

We plunged into "Hark, the Herald Angels Sing" and concluded our service.

As I put away the communion vessels, Bernie said, "I haven't had communion in such a long time. This has been a blessing. I didn't know I had this surprise in store for me today."

Neither did I, Bernie. Neither did I.

Chapter 3

Family Tree

What if Jesus submitted his DNA for genetic testing? Is divine DNA traceable?

Jesus's human family tree is outlined in the gospels of Matthew and Luke. One genealogy takes Jesus's ancestry back to Abraham, and the other connects the dots all the way to Adam.

My maternal grandparents were third cousins. My grandmother called her mother-in-law "Cousin Betty." This may explain our family traits of absent-mindedness and eleven toes. I enjoy watching Henry Louis Gates Jr. peel back the pages of celebrity family history on the television show *"Finding Your Roots*. It is remarkable what dates and names from census documents, ship logs, and tax archives can uncover.

My forbear, Joseph Gray, served as a soldier in the Maryland militia so I qualify as a daughter of the American Revolution. Matthew and Luke each do a good bit of namedropping in Jesus's genealogy. They both claim that Jesus is a descendant of several Old Testament muckety-mucks: Abraham, Isaac, Jacob, David, Solomon.

According to the Torah, Jewishness is matrilineal. Only the child of a Jewish woman is considered to be truly Jewish. This was likely to discourage Jewish men from taking foreign wives and to protect Jewish women from neglect. So it is all the more interesting that the only two women named in Jesus's ancestry are both foreigners. Jesus's ancestor Rahab ran a house of ill repute in Jericho. Apparently, she married one of the men who entered the city after its wall toppled. Ruth, the great-grandmother of King David, was a Moabite, and the only non-Jew whose name is given to a book of the bible.

Of the twelve tribes of Israel, Jesus is descended from the tribe of Judah. This is surprising. Joseph was the favorite son who got the special coat, and his story takes up more chapters of Genesis than any of the other patriarchs. But Joseph is not Jesus's venerable grandpappy. Judah, not the flashy Joseph, is the brother who gets the nod and can draw a straight line to Jesus.

Judah was the fourth of twelve brothers, and his name means "Praise the Lord." There are stories in Genesis that indicate Judah was a stand-up guy. He stops his brothers from committing murder, and when he suspects that his youngest brother is about to be enslaved, he offers to take his place.

But there is a story of Judah that makes my kissing cousin grandparents look tame. Through a wild and bewildering turn of events by today's standards and mores, Judah impregnates his widowed daughter-in-law, Tamar, with twins, one of whom extends the family tree to Jesus. (Genesis 38)

What is deemed righteous can change from one culture to another, from one generation to another. That Jesus's family tree has less than pristine laundry hanging on it makes me like him even more. Every family tree is checkered with heroes and zeros. Mine included. Though I was exaggerating about eleven toes, we have deviated from the norm from time to time.

Some of my favorite relatives are the ones who married into the family. My Aunt Flo got her Ph.D. in chemistry in 1953 and was a lifelong learner and teacher. At her daughter's sixtieth birthday party, Aunt Flo, at eighty-nine years old, put together a PowerPoint slideshow to share! My two brothers-in-law add energy, humor and stability to our family, proving that my sisters' and my ability to choose a husband ranks as our best family trait.

It could be said that Joseph married into the holy family. Though Jesus technically might have been biologically related only to his mother,

Joseph has an under-recognized but impressive impact upon the young Messiah.

In the city of Montreal, I visited a beautiful church. Above the altar in the church is a statue of a figure cradling the baby Jesus. It is not a typical Madonna and child statue; the central figure over the altar is a man holding the Christ Child. The church is St. Joseph's Basilica. Joseph is flanked by two angels, and over far to his left is a solitary statue of Mary, his wife.

It is unusual to see Joseph given the place of honor in any artistic rendition of the holy family. He is usually a supporting actor only. In most Christmas pageants, Joseph has no lines to say, and is merely Mary's bathrobe-clad escort, standing quietly in her shadow. I do remember one Christmas pageant, however, when Joseph was forced to play a larger role. The baby Jesus that year was not meek and mild, but screeched throughout the entire pageant. The child playing Mary handed the bawling infant over to the boy playing Joseph. The young Joseph, looking stricken, jiggled the crying Jesus for as long as he could stand it, and then passed the hot potato of a baby over to the angel Gabriel.

Much is made over Mary being visited by an angel, but an angel appears to Joseph in his dreams not once, not twice, but on four separate occasions. Time and time again, Joseph is asked to do what might seem irrational or imprudent, but Joseph trusts that God knows what he is doing.

Joseph disappears early in the gospels, but through the stories his son tells, perhaps we learn what kind of man and father he was. In five of Jesus's parables, a father is the central character, and in each, the father is depicted as either loving, forgiving, just, or concerned about his children's welfare. Like Disney, Jesus tells no parable with a mother in the story, even in a minor role. The father in the parable of the Prodigal Son is probably the most famous father in Jesus's stories. In that story we see a gentle, big-hearted man. Are we being given a glimpse here of the sort of father Joseph was?

In prayer, Jesus calls God "Abba," which means "Daddy." (Mark 14:36) But surely he first called Joseph "Abba." Jesus uses the metaphor of a human father-child relationship to describe his own divine relationship with God and encourages his disciples to know God as their Father. Could Jesus have spoken of fathers and father-child relationships so often and in such realistic, positive terms without having a deeply meaningful experience somewhere along the way with his own father? Joseph is most likely the man who gave Jesus the sense that fatherhood is a glorious reality that mirrored both the strength and tenderness of God.

Joseph essentially adopts Jesus and must have endured social ridicule for the gossip-rich circumstances of the boy's birth. Joseph's *largesse*, his willingness to embrace and protect his odd little family, is worthy of more recognition than it usually receives. The charming and beloved story of Jesus being born in a barn following a long journey had to have been a nightmare for Joseph. Mary and the baby Jesus are given such exalted status that we tend to overlook the enormous burden that Joseph endured.

All burdens imply heaviness but sometimes heft and density point to significance and substance—that which matters and means the most. Some obligations weigh us down and keep us grounded. Other burdens are the very things that enable us to fly, like the burden of wings on the back of a bird, or the burden of a sail to the mast of a boat. Christ who comes to relieve our burdens enters this world as a burden to Joseph, yet if we read between the lines of the gospels, we might be able to see how Joseph's burden gave way to his deepest joy.

Jesus's family tree was crowded with the revered and the reviled, the same sort of folks he encountered and embraced throughout his life. His understanding of family was not limited to bloodlines. He called a woman shunned by her community "daughter," his disciples "my brothers," and anyone who did the will of God his "mother." (Mark 5:34, Matthew 28:10, Luke 8:21)

Jesus's family tree includes a branch for everyone because somewhere along the way, whether from nature or nurture, God's DNA shows up in all of us.

PERICOPE (2020)

Mary's Chapel Missionary Baptist Church in Scotland Neck, North Carolina, is a small white clapboard church.

The church is not named for the mother of Jesus. It is named for Mary Barnes, who was born enslaved and served the household of my eastern North Carolina relatives for sixty years. Mary Barnes had one daughter, Virginia, who moved to Petersburg to work and save money after the Civil War. Virginia died long before turning gray, and her mother inherited her child's life savings. Mary Barnes chose to use the money to build a church for "the use of her race," as the family history book records it. The book also refers to Mary Barnes as the family's "black mammy." Mary Barnes died in 1889.

During the pandemic, the pastor of Mary's Chapel stood outside the front doors, and members of the congregation sat in their cars and listened to his sermon. He encouraged them to honk their car horns when they heard some good news in his sermon. I watched the service online, and there was a lot of honking while he preached.

Racism is not just embedded in systems but in me as well—in ways that sometimes I recognize, reject, and repair, but also in ways I don't realize. In 1789 my ancestor owned seventy-eight slaves. Their names, such as Gilpap, Quash, Annekey, and Tokiah, indicate that they were born in Africa. Each generation of my family since has been a land and homeowner, right up to and including me and my family. My great-great-great-grandfather went to college, and every descendant of his up to me and my family attended college too. Economic and educational advantages were readily available and taken.

Mary Barnes's legacy is a little chapel where the story of Jesus has been preached and hope has been served up for more than a century. The love, care, and faith she shared with my ancestors when they were babies and children perhaps has passed down to me in some way too.

Something old is falling apart (thank God), and something new and generous and fair is being raised up that will challenge me to relinquish, to give over, and to empty myself of assumptions, privileges, and inequities that have long benefited me at an exorbitant price to others.

In the Episcopal church we proclaim the mystery of faith, saying: *Christ has died, Christ is risen, Christ will come again.* (Book of Common Prayer, page 363) We are saying we believe that the deconstruction, the death, the loss of any and all things is also the precursor, the catalyst, and the herald of growth, life, and new beginnings. We declare that such is always the order. Death is never last. Life always follows. And for that kind of good news, we all ought to lay on the horn.

Chapter 4

Boy Wonder

I bet Mary loved to tell the story.

There is only one story in the bible about Jesus between the ages of two and thirty. Perhaps the story endured because Jesus's mother kept it alive. I am guilty of showing baby pictures of my son to his girlfriend and regaling her with stories of his exasperating, sweet adolescent years. Moms haven't changed much.

Jesus is twelve, so the story goes, and he has one foot in childhood and the other in adulthood. Along with other travelers, he and his family make an annual sixty-mile trek from Nazareth to Jerusalem for Passover. Jesus goes to the temple and has a remarkable tête-à-tête with the religious eggheads. Jesus's understanding of the Law astounds them, and Jesus gets so embroiled in conversation at the temple he loses track of time. He forgets to rejoin his parents, and the caravan of pilgrims head back home without him.

Halfway to Nazareth, the blood drains out of Mary and Joseph's faces. "I thought he was with you!"

They turn around and, on the way, imagine every worst-case scenario. They find Jesus in the temple, unaware that he has caused any turmoil. He shows no remorse when they tell him of their panic. Quite possibly, he rolls his eyes. "Why were you looking for me? Didn't you know it was necessary for me to be in my Father's house?" (Luke 2:49)

It is reassuring to realize that teenagers have always been problematic. One intellectual described his experience:

Youth today loves luxury. They have bad manners, contempt for authority, no respect for older people, and talk nonsense when they should work. Young people do not stand up any longer when adults enter the room. They contradict their parents, talk too much in company, guzzle their food, and tyrannize their elders.[3]

The author? Socrates in the fifth century BC.

Jesus was a bright boy. He was from a small, insignificant village in a time when the literacy rate was three percent or lower. He must have been singled out early for possessing prodigious potential. His family was poor and could not have paid for an elite education, but the story of him in the temple at twelve suggests that he received the sort of advanced education afforded to only a few.

I asked a group of twelve-year-old Sunday schoolers to act out the story, ad-libbing the dialogue. Stuart Castillo assumed the role of Joseph finding Jesus in the temple.

"We were worried about you," he said with no emotion or inflection.

"Stuart," I said. "Is this the way your father speaks when he is upset with you? Imagine how Joseph is feeling by the time he finds Jesus and try again."

Stuart looked at me, reentered the scene, and did not disappoint.

"Jesus H. Christ! What were you thinking?" The class roared.

I like to review the story of Jesus at age twelve with students the same age. The story is instructive for several reasons. It highlights both Jesus's divinity (his brilliant mind and draw to the temple) and his humanity

---

3   Attributed to Socrates by Plato, according to William L. Patty and Louise S. Johnson, *Personality and Adjustment,* p. 277 (1953)

(his lack of consideration for his parents). Jesus's exchange of ideas at the temple suggests that as early as age twelve we have within us the budding signs of our particular strengths and passions. Missing the caravan home points to the fact that abilities often develop before good judgment does, and the palpable tension when Mary and Joseph find him illustrates the unsettling but unavoidable break from parents that must happen for a child to become an adult.

Coupled with this story, I ask the class: at what age do you think a child can physically manipulate a pair of scissors properly?

Once we establish that by age two or three most children can cut paper with scissors, I ask why we give children blunted scissors and not a sharp pair.

This exercise is a set up. When they explain to me that a developing child's cognitive ability does not always keep up with his or her physical capacity, I come in with what the SAT once used to torture teens: an analogy. It's also a trap.

We don't give a two or three-year-old sharp scissors because while their hands can move the blades to cut, their brains can't grasp the danger, and they could unwittingly and unintentionally hurt themselves or someone else. Likewise, teenagers may feel they are ready for intimate relationships, but their cerebral cortexes are still maturing, and they could unwittingly and unintentionally hurt themselves or someone else.

Cue the eye-rolling, but I had their attention.

Jesus wasn't finished growing up at twelve and still needed his parents. Very few teenagers know better than their parents.

But don't despair, the tide will turn, I tell them. One day you will possess the better judgment and need to say to a parent, "It's time for you to stop driving. Hand over your keys."

The story of Jesus the child/man in the temple is a foreshadowing of how Jesus will deftly hold contradictions in tension and call his followers to do the same.

Jesus tells us that we receive by giving. We lead by serving. We are made new by dying. Suffering and love are two sides of the same coin. Grief and gratitude are lashed together. Sadness stems from the sources of our joy. Faith is called forth from what we cannot know or control. Wounds turn into scars but also empathy and healing. Forgiving someone releases us from our own pain. Peace is possible in a raging storm. The lost and the least and the last are the Christ among us.

We grow in spiritual maturity as we become more agile in dealing with mystery and mayhem. The more we can gather our arms around paradox and dueling dualities, the wiser and kinder and more Christlike we become. Grace finds a welcome within us and through us.

The cross is far away when Jesus dazzles the temple authorities, but the shape of that cross, stretching and spanning to reach all possibilities, is coming into view.

PERICOPE (2009)

My mothering and athletic coaching sometimes are at odds.

My daughter, Julia Gray, plays first base for her high school softball team, and when the first base coach for the opposing team was hit hard by a ball, Julia Gray rushed to his side. While I beamed from the bleachers, Julia Gray's coach was about to come out of his skin from the dugout, screaming for Julia Gray to tag out the runner who stood a foot off the bag, also concerned about the injured coach.

On senior day, when Julia Gray, a junior, was replaced by a senior, I was proud that she didn't pout on the bench the whole game. She was happy to see her teammate play well. The coach saw it differently. "I hear you didn't *want* to get in the game," he sneered the next day.

Her coach also frowns on laughter in the dugout when the team is trailing—losers should not be enjoying themselves.

The ballfield is rife with life lessons for living out our faith. Jesus frequently stands at odds with the world's coaching. Jesus hangs out with losers, and tells stories about how loss and losing are the only true way to win. To signify losers, kids today form their hand into the shape of the letter L and place it over their forehead. I was with our eighth-grade church school class last Sunday, and one student joked that the L over his forehead stood for love, not loser. Precisely, Jesus might say.

It's good to question what coach you are listening to lately, and also what sort of coaching you are providing for others. My daughter and her softball teammates won fewer than half their games, and I am proud to say they are a very fine group of losers.

Chapter 5

UFO Sighting

My husband, Tim, taught first-grade Sunday school, and on Saturday night he began looking for an arts and crafts project for the children to do the next morning. The Sunday lesson was on the baptism of Jesus. Being fairly craft challenged myself, I helped by googling "baptism of Jesus craft." I was surprised by what I found.

The search yielded websites that claim a UFO was sighted at Jesus's baptism.

The bible reports that when Jesus was baptized the heavens opened and the Spirit of God descended like a dove. Mark's gospel goes on to say that after the baptism, the Spirit *drove* Jesus into the wilderness. So, as uforc.com tells it, the heavens opened and an unidentified solid flying object descended from the sky with a flight characteristic similar to that of a dove. This wing-shaped spacecraft came to rest above Jesus, took him aboard, and drove him into the wilderness.

Now admittedly, that version of the story would have made for a neat craft idea involving paper plates that a first-grader would love. Can't you just see Jesus smiling out the window of a flying saucer?

The baptism of Jesus and all baptisms do have a certain otherworldliness about them. Is it science fiction or fantasy that we believe baptism makes any difference?

Compared to the Mississippi River, the Jordan River looks like a "crick." A fallen tree trunk could easily traverse it. At the site where Jesus's baptism is said to have taken place, Israel and the country Jordan are in spitting distance from one another. Walking through the water from one riverbank to the other side would take only seconds, if not for the fence in the middle of the river that separates the two nations. People wade into the water on both sides of the banks to be baptized at the presumed place where John the Baptist set up shop and dunked Jesus. To arrive there, cars and buses stick to a narrow road through a colorless, desolate landscape littered with live landmines left over from the Six Days War.

Thirty miles up the river is an easily accessible and friendly tourist center complete with a gift shop, robes, towels, and showers where thousands come each year to get in the water. When my colleague, the Reverend Matt Holcombe, and I stood in this popular juncture of the Jordan, we locked eyes as minnows nibbled at our feet. We silently agreed not to mention it to those we'd invited to fall back in our arms under the cold river to reaffirm their baptismal covenant.

When John the Baptist plunged folks under the muddy waters of the Jordan River, it was serious business. Jews were not in the practice of being baptized. Baptisms were required of converts to Judaism, as was circumcision—ergo, conversion was not taken lightly. A Jew inherited the promise of Abraham and didn't need a baptism of repentance or new birth. But John the Baptist disagreed, believing that spiritual lives had become so dead that Jews also needed to undergo the ritual.

John draws the proverbial line in the sand. A hard line. He is a man of exaggerations. He takes on an ascetic, self-punishing lifestyle that may have given him the gall to lambast the religious elite. No one is exempt from his censure. John blisters King Herod for numerous vile deeds including stealing his brother's wife—a reproach that eventually costs John his head. Yet John's preaching has great appeal. Soldiers, pharisees, tax collectors, and fishermen flock to hear John's alarming assessment of their eternal future and to be soaked in the Jordan. John attracts loyal disciples yet asserts that he is just a forerunner. The real deal is on his heels.

John insists that the coming Messiah is so far superior that John isn't worthy to untie the man's shoes. If locust-eating, hair shirt–wearing, shame-throwing, king-bashing John the Baptist doesn't think he is worth much standing next to the Messiah, imagine how everyone else thought they would size up against the man.

John and Jesus are on the same team but have opposite approaches. John fasts and Jesus feasts. John preaches a grim justice; Jesus speaks of love and forgiveness. John expects people to come to him in the desert. Jesus goes into the towns and villages to meet people. John harps "Repent." Jesus hums "Be not afraid."

John is astonished when Jesus asks to be baptized. Only sinners are baptized. John points his finger at Jesus and proclaims him to be the long-awaited Messiah. But Jesus lines up not with the righteous and holy but among the wrecked, shamed, and outcast to wade into the Jordan. He honors John with the task of baptizing him.

If a room full of first-graders were asked who is good at arts and crafts, every hand in the room would shoot up into the air. At six years old we think we are fine artists, but before we finish elementary school, few of us still believe it. Sometimes the same thing happens to our faith in God and in ourselves. When we are small, we can believe that God loves us. Who doesn't? But somewhere along the line, the idea loses credibility. Either we lose confidence in our own "loveableness" or we lose faith that God's love can do much for us. In other words, so what if God loves us? What good is that?

The outrageous claim of baptism is that not only does God love us, but God's love has the power to do things we long for: to heal, forgive, resurrect, make new, rebuild, give peace, foster hope, instill purpose, and create communities of trust and joy. That may sound like sci-fi, but it is the Christian faith. It is real, or folks are wasting their time on Jesus.

A family adopted three children. The children had a difficult time adjusting. They were suspicious, withdrawn, and humorless. Numerous foster homes had made them so. Soon after the children joined the family, an abandoned dog also was taken in. The dog proved to be good-natured but poorly disciplined. The three adopted children each began to connect positively with the dog in a way that none of them did with any of the family members.

One afternoon, the mother of this clan was in the kitchen cooking with the children nearby when one asked, "Is our dog foster or adopted?"

The mother stopped stirring. She turned and faced the child. "Adopted," she answered. "This means we're not just looking after her. She's ours. She's family."

"Even if she's bad, you won't send her away?" the child asked.

"Never."

"You won't hurt her?" the child went on.

"Never," the mother said again.

After a moment, the child said, "We're adopted."

"Yes, you are," the mother said, her eyes filling with tears.[4]

Every soul belongs to God, and earth is our adopted home. As the author of Hebrews writes, we are strangers here and desire a better country, a heavenly one. Our native land is abroad.

Ghoulish language is used in the Episcopal baptismal service and hardly noticed: In baptism "We are buried with Christ in his death. By it we share in his resurrection." (*Book of Common Prayer*, page 306) A baptism reenacts Jesus's death and resurrection. The notion that babies are buried, even drowned, at baptism—symbolic or not—is repugnant,

---

4   I was unable to recall or find the source of this story.

even monstrous. So we gussy up the occasions with lacy gowns followed by brunch.

Yet baptism is death to a certain way of life. Parents of baptized children renounce "powers of this world which corrupt and destroy." (*BCP*, page 302) At an American naturalization ceremony, immigrants renounce previous loyalty to any "prince or potentate" and pledge allegiance to serve and protect the United States. Likewise, baptism sets terms for Christian citizenship: remain engaged in a community of faith, resist evil, ask for forgiveness after screwing up, resemble Jesus in word and deed, serve others as kindly as you would want to be served, and roll up your sleeves to provide plentiful hope and honor for all people.

The Greek word *baptizo* has been found in written recipes that are older than Jesus. In ancient cooking recipes, *to baptize* means to immerse the ingredient in a solution over time—which we call pickling.[5] To baptize in the kitchen means not simply to dip an ingredient once but to immerse it continuously so that the ingredient is transformed. Though it is true that we believe in the need for only one formal baptism, we also believe in the need for ongoing worship, community, scripture, prayer, applied faith, and service. A baptism is not a dunk and dash. It is more like marinating. We are called to immerse ourselves in the ways of Jesus over a lifetime so that we might become more and more Christlike.

Jesus's baptism inaugurates a campaign to build up lives for the good of all. There is consistency in his message from start to finish. From the get-go, Jesus's ministry is about lifting people up, identifying with their brokenness, and reconciling them with God.

It is nearly impossible to see an immediate difference in a child who's been baptized. Yet my colleague, the Reverend Verdery Kerr, calls it a stunning moment when parents hand their child to the priest for baptism. The parents acknowledge that the child is not theirs but God's.

---

5   *Bible Study Magazine*, James Montgomery Boice, May 1989

When the priest gives the child back to the parents, God proclaims that the child is the parents' for safekeeping.

Baptism is intended to be as it was for Jesus: a watershed moment, a sea change, a stake jammed into the dirt. Jesus hears the words, "You are my son, the beloved. With you I am well pleased." (Mark 1:11) We seek to offer those same words to anyone we baptize and to be bearers of those words of grace to all.

Love alone awakens love, as Pearl Buck wrote. Knowing that we matter awakens us to what matters. At a baptism, somehow, someway, God's adoption of us—God's pleasure in us—turns our hearts to him, like a flower that cannot help but turn toward the sun. A baptism is not a *naming* ceremony but a *claiming* ceremony. God claims us as his own, and gives us the option of spending the rest of our lives claiming him right back.

Every baptism is a sign of God's mysterious, exaggerated, otherworldly movement. Climb aboard, alien.

Pericope (2021)

One year I gave up yelling at my children for Lent.

They were ten, eight, and four. My volume control was no longer under control. I raised my voice far too often, making none of us happy. I told our children the plan. They were thrilled and took great pleasure in holding me accountable.

Of all the Lenten disciplines I have taken on through the years, this one stuck. I broke a bad habit. I had been yelling because no one seemed to listen to me. As it turned out, the less I yelled, the more they heard me. I got better at listening to them too.

It surprised me to realize that being good at listening is not just about hearing what someone says. It's also about how my listening makes someone else *feel.*

Listening has restorative powers. Some pain cannot be taken away, but hurt that is heard can be eased. When someone listens to us with a desire to understand and appreciate, we unfurl and expand. The woman who touched the hem of Jesus's garment was healed of her disease. She also got to tell Jesus "the whole truth." That he listened to her story likely healed her soul as well.

My two favorite Lents were those when I was on maternity leave. I didn't take on any special Lenten practice, although I sacrificed sleep and sanity all forty days. I spent those Lents falling in love, nestling a grapefruit-sized head against my heart. I am spending this Lent nuzzling the head of my infant grandson. I am listening for his fretful cries, contented coos, and still, small voice. If I am quiet, I can hear the love between us flowing like a rushing river.

CHAPTER 6

BOW AND ARROW

WHEN MY CHILDREN were young, I read a picture book to them that told the true story of three-year-old Sarah Wilcher, who gets lost in the New Hampshire woods in 1783. Her family and neighbors search for her day and night. A man dreams that Sarah is being protected by a bear. When she is found safe and well beneath a tree, bear tracks encircle her.[6]

The story makes me rethink a small detail included in Mark's terse telling of the temptations. Mark doesn't mention the specific tests, only that when they were over, Jesus "was with the wild beasts and the angels waited upon him." (Mark 1:13) Perhaps the wild animals were not threats but also sources of protection and comfort like the angels.

The temptation story is unique in the gospels because it is a story that only Jesus could have told. There are no human witnesses to his forty-day ordeal.

The bible often associates "forty" with testing. Like Jesus, Moses and Elijah fasted for forty days. The Israelites wandered in the desert for forty years. Goliath later harassed them for forty days before David finally beaned him. The Torah forbids scourging someone beyond forty lashes. The word *quarantine* is derived from the word meaning "forty." Forty indicates a period of proving as well as improving.

The most famous "forty" biblical story is that of Noah and the ark. (Genesis 7-9) It is one of the first bible stories told to children, and

---

6   *The Bear That Heard Crying* by Natalie Kinsey-Warnock and Helen Kinsey, copyright 1997.

unlike it did for Sarah, the tale of the ark does not end well for most people. Though Noah and his family, along with a select pairing of the animal kingdom, are saved, the story of the flood is a tale of genocide at the hands of God. Children's bibles gloss over that part.

"Forty" bible stories are often splattered with violence. They are battles against fear and despair, and the temptation to respond to evil with our fists. The ark and the flood are God's first stab at reacting to massive-scale evil gone amok. God chooses violence, wiping out every disobedient creature except who is sealed up in the ark. It is fitting that evil is "live" spelled backward. Evil works to undo life, unraveling and reversing any movement toward human flourishing, any path to justice or goodness.

When my daughters were three and one, the older child, Caroline, clobbered her sister. In a flash, I smacked Caroline while saying, "Don't hit your sister!" The irony made me vow not to hit my children again. I know of two more times that I did. Caroline both times. First children put up with a lot.

God appears to have the same epiphany that I did. When the flood is over, God puts a bow in the sky. The word "rainbow" is not in the story of Noah and the ark. Rainbows are found only in the Book of Revelation when describing heavenly images (Revelation 4:3, 10:1). The "bow" in the story of the flood is the kind that sends an arrow flying.

God hangs up his bow in the clouds. A bow, a weapon, is turned into a symbol of peace and hope, like a sword into a plowshare or like how another instrument of death—the cross—is later transformed. God makes a covenant with every living creature to never flood the earth again, seeming to have learned that as tempting as it is, responding to evil with violence does not remove it. As if offering corroboration, when Noah gets off the ark, he mortifies himself before his children by drinking until he blacks out naked in his tent.

When the devil confronts Jesus in the wilderness, the temptation for Jesus is to do violence to his soul—to satisfy his belly and betray his principles, to exploit and grandstand his relationship with God, to wield power *over* people instead of *for* people.

We are told that the devil shows up at the end of the forty days of fasting when Jesus is starving. Not hungry. Starving. People who are starving cannot think or act clearly. Yes, Jesus was human and divine, but if his divinity diminishes his human experience, then he was not truly human but only pretending to be. Jesus's human experience includes some of the most intense physical, mental, and spiritual pain and anguish possible. His divinity does not negate or lessen his humanity. His divinity opens his humanity to reveal the grace, strength, generosity, and courage that is inherent and possible for all human life.

When I was four and my sister Cobey was eight, we quarreled so much that our mother decided the worst punishment she could give us would be to confine us together in one room for a day. She brought our meals to us on a tray. The result was that Cobey and I got along famously that day and thought the room service was wonderful. I don't know if our mother was frustrated or delighted by our response. I wonder if God had punishment or reconciliation in mind when he called for hawks and doves, lambs and lions, and pigs and peacocks to be shut up in the ark together. Genesis says it was God who closed the door behind them, probably feeling the same way my mother did when she banished my sister and me to the room for a day.

I read the story of Noah and the ark, and the temptations of Jesus, as myths instead of actual events. They are myths that reveal truth about God, Jesus, and you and me. The divine team is not in a separate dugout, but always and infinitely on our side. God is in this for the long haul no matter how despicably we behave, and violence is off the table. In the desert, Jesus puts on a clinic. Yes, we will be tempted to degrade ourselves and others for the illusion of lifting ourselves up. But as God learns in the story of the flood and as Jesus demonstrates in the desert, there is a holier and better way.

In the movie *The Lion King*, the lion prince is visited by his father's spirit, who says to him, "You are more than you have become."

Starting with the temptations, Jesus shows what more we can become.

Pericope (2018)

We were told it had cost $2,500 to repair its broken wing and rehabilitate the bird, and now it was moments from freedom and flight. For Christmas I got my husband the opportunity to release a raptor, courtesy of the Carolina Raptor Center. One Sunday in January a red-shouldered hawk was brought in a box to our backyard. The hawk had been found one hundred days earlier with a broken wing. After surgery and rehab, where it proved it could fly in confinement and catch live prey, the hawk was ready to sail the skies again.

My husband opened the box. The hawk did not move. He tipped the box on its side. The hawk still did not move. Its wing was healed and the way cleared—what remained was remembering what it was born to do. The hawk stayed inside the box long enough for us to get a good look at it and take pictures. Then with a deep shudder of its wings, it hurtled out of the box and into a neighbor's tall pine tree, and then to the top of an even higher tree. It looked around for a while, as if surveying and getting its bearings, and then it was gone.

The price of fixing one hawk's wing was high. But I love the care, devotion, and expense given to one of God's creatures who will never say thank you or fathom the cost of the gift. It is enough to see it fly, to see it do what it was made to do.

Repairing broken wings is a lot of what the church's ministry is about. There are people nursing broken wings all around us. Maybe your own wing is in a sling right now. It is a gift to enable flight, to help one another to spread their wings. In our homes and in the places where we work and serve, there are also broken wings we can help mend. There are boxes we can open, releasing potential and creativity. And it will be enough.

Chapter 7

The Sidekicks

I HAVE A theory about the twelve disciples. I'm willing to bet that a number of them were teenagers.

Artists usually render the disciples as grizzled, bearded old men, but it could be that some of them were just *starting* to shave.

Scripture tells us that most of the twelve spontaneously follow Jesus. James and John leave their father sitting slack-jawed in a fishing boat. That they are still working for their father gives us a hint about their age, and who else but teenagers would have jumped up to follow Jesus without concern for responsibilities and obligations?

Peter is the only disciple we know for certain is married. Perhaps the others have no wife or child to care for, aren't set in their ways or jaded by past disappointments, and are free to take up and follow Jesus.

On more than one occasion, the disciples argue, complain, or ask questions that embarrass themselves. Jesus's message often flies right over their heads. They are still concrete thinkers. Their cerebral cortex isn't finished developing. It is in the nature of teenagers to do what is impulsive and to want to try new things. For instance, body piercing parlors report that hardly anyone over twenty-four comes in to get their tongue pierced.

An adolescent's open mind, impulsivity, and willingness to experience new and different things make them ripe for following a barrier-breaking, authority-defying miracle maker who had a reputation for enjoying good food and wine. Jesus was catnip for bored teenagers with dreams of glory.

Two disciples, James and John, ask a favor of Jesus that outrages the other ten. James and John, like campaign staffers jockeying for cabinet positions before the election, request the honor of being seated at Jesus's right and left hand when he hits the big time. James and John expect Jesus's kingdom to be an earthly one, otherwise they might not have gotten out of their father's boat so quickly. The literacy rate among Galilean fisherman was five percent. Opportunities to move up the ladder were rare but ambition was not.

The twelve are not cookie-cutter disciples but represent a varied group, from Simon the Zealot, a trigger-happy firebrand eager to oust the Romans, to Matthew the tax collector who collaborates with the Romans. But why no women among the twelve?

Like teenagers, first-century women have more incentive to follow Jesus, but for opposite reasons. Teens are rash and unburdened. The women who follow Jesus are weighed down with obligation and limited options. Their interest in Jesus and his message didn't have anything to do with adventure or glory, but freedom and respect.

In ancient Judaism, men and women were not permitted to speak to one another in public; they were separated during worship. Women were not educated, could be divorced without cause, and were considered too unreliable to serve as witnesses in court. Jesus challenges these restrictions on a number of occasions. He speaks directly to several women in public settings (the woman at the well, the widow of Nain, the woman with the hemorrhage, the woman caught in adultery, the woman with the crooked back) and in private homes (Mary and Martha, the Syrophoenician woman, the woman who anoints him). He teaches women and condemns divorces on frivolous grounds that leave women destitute. The indisputable first witness of the resurrection is a woman.

In Luke 8:1-2, we are told that several women follow Jesus, including Joanna and Susanna, who are named as angel investors, bankrolling Jesus's ministry. (Thank you, Luke, for adding this throwaway line in your gospel that explains so much!) When the twelve abandon Jesus at his arrest, his mother, Mary, and Mary of Magda remain ardent disciples and are beside him in his last days and last hours.

Jesus preaches traditionally feminine values of vulnerability, nonviolence, love, and compassion, which, in his era, had a stronger impact, greater authority, and stood out more as a different path when affirmed by male disciples than they would coming from women. Oppressed women and teenagers were the most likely to be attracted to Jesus's message, to be drawn to a movement that challenged unjust systems and provided the vision of a better future.

When Jesus feeds the multitude, the crowd is recorded as "five thousand, not counting women and children." Women not only were discounted as peers to men, they were literally *not counted*. The bible reports that Jesus had several women disciples, but it was not the custom of the men who told his story to include or regard women as worthy of being counted. Besides, "twelve" has such a nice ring to it since there were twelve tribes of Israel.

Women and teenagers, considered lightweights in the first century, might have made up the core and the majority of the original disciples. Perhaps the later call of the highly educated Paul is meant to provide the movement with gravitas.

I was ordained one month after turning twenty-six. I wasn't a teenager, but I possessed no gravitas. Sometimes I wonder how I ended up being a priest. I opened a door, and it led to another door, and so it went until a bishop laid his hand on my hand, and *voila*, I was ordained and the next door awaited me. As a child and teen, I never aspired to be a minister. But perhaps there were a few hints to my future.

I sang in the choir as a child. My two best friends sang with me, and when we took our choir robes home to be cleaned, we played an unusual form of dress up. Fairley and I put a pillowcase on our heads to look like a nun's wimple. She and I transformed into Sister Alden and Sister Maurice, while Angus became Father John. Fairley is an attorney and Angus is a playwright and screenwriter. One Christmas, Fairley gave me a ceramic nun that was a music box. The nun went round and round to the tune of "Dominique."

In addition to the choir, I was an acolyte and active in Sunday school and teenage Christian groups. I asked for a bible for Christmas when I was twelve. My freshman year of college, I chose to take Introduction to the Old Testament for my elective course. I got an "A," so I kept taking more religion classes until it was one of my majors by my junior year.

I was drawn to Jesus but I have never been very good at praying or being especially kind or unselfish. I like to be liked too much, and maybe I wanted God to like me too. I am inspired to follow Jesus because of all the times Jesus has followed me. He has stuck by me more than I him. As it ends up, I am better at telling other people how to be a disciple than being a disciple myself. I know way too many people who were never ordained who are much better followers of Jesus than I am, like Winston, Henry, Jim, Muriel, Aimee, Alice, and Scott.

From the start, the unremarkable and the irreverent are as likely to follow Jesus as the distinguished and devout. Thank God, because it's a great gig. Teenagers can't have all the fun.

PERICOPE (2005)

My daughter will be eighteen in a few days, which is amazing since I was eighteen only a few years ago myself. As I reflect on my hopes for this adult daughter of mine, the words of our liturgies in the church from the *Book of Common Prayer* come to mind.

"You are sealed by the Holy Spirit in baptism and marked as Christ's own forever." (page 308) The Reverend Henry Parsley said these words when he thumbed the sign of the cross on my daughter's infant forehead. Eighteen years in our home is not forever, and though the years have gone like the proverbial blink of an eye, I am comforted that she belongs to someone forever. And that someone loves her perfectly and completely and unendingly, as I might have hoped I could.

"Strengthen you in all goodness…" (page 360) We say these words after we confess our sins each week in worship. There is much in the world that can weaken and fragment us, maybe even especially for a young woman. We might be made tougher and stronger by our mistakes, failures, and disappointments, but I have more trust in the forces of goodness to strengthen her for life's work.

"Empower her for your service …" (page 418) Bishop Gary Gloster said when he laid his hands upon her teenage head at confirmation. These days she knows more about what she *doesn't* want to do than what she *wants* to do. Whatever develops and reveals itself to be her path, I hope she recognizes that serving Christ can happen anywhere.

"In your infinite love, you made us for yourself." (page 362) We hear these words as part of the Eucharistic Great Thanksgiving. I sometimes think my daughter was made just for me, but she is really God's glory.

"Send us out to do the work you have given us to do," (page 366) we pray at the close of the Eucharist. It was the plan from the moment she was born that one day she would leave us. For Tim and me, she was the work given to us, and we will send her forth, knowing God will have work for her to do that will bring her the joy we have known in ours.

The Jewish word for "life" is spelled with the eighth and tenth letter in the Hebrew alphabet, so eighteen is considered a lucky number. So be it, my daughter, so be it.

CHAPTER 8

JESUS AND CHRIST

A QUESTION IN seminary scrambled my mind. Are Jesus and Christ the same?

I was surprised. It seemed like asking if Lisa Saunders is the same as Lisa and Saunders. But then again, my name at birth was Elizabeth Goodwin. I took on a nickname and a married name. My names vary, but I am the same. Or *am* I?

Is there a difference between Jesus and Christ? It depends upon how you break it down.

A holy host of theologians have shaped my Christology. (Their names are listed at the end of the chapter.)

This is how I break it down.

Christ is "scratch and smell," "taste and see" God. Saint Paul says "He is the image of the invisible God." (Colossians 1:15) Christ is the union of the divine and matter. The Big Bang could be called the invisible God exploding into the visible.

Christ is the Greek word for "Messiah" or "the anointed." Christ was present from the start, from *the* genesis. As we say in the Nicene Creed, "through him all things were made." The gospel of John reads, "he was in the beginning with God." (John 1:2)

Christ anoints all creation with the sacred presence of the Creator. Christ is God revealed in mud and star, leaf and surf, fur and fin. All of creation is drenched, steeped, saturated in Christ. Franciscan priest Richard Rohr says we live in a "Christ-soaked world."[7] The prophet Isaiah writes that trees clap their hands, and mountains and hills burst into song in glory to God. (Isaiah 55:12)

The baby Jesus of Nazareth was born two thousand years ago and was not at creation. Christ was.

The violet backed starling, a field of bluebonnets, a guileless golden retriever, or the Mediterranean Turquoise Coast might also be Christ-filled, but they are not human.

We needed a human Christ. We got Jesus Christ. Touchable. Relatable. Comprehendible.

God came to earth in Jesus of Nazareth, but God was already here. Jesus is God in the flesh and provides a pure (in the sense of undiluted and untainted) revelation of God that humans can understand. He also serves as a spiritual Sherpa. We can follow Jesus to become purely ourselves. Jesus is the Christ, but the Christ is not Jesus alone.

Growing up I heard that Jesus Christ died for my sins. By his blood, he paid my debt. This puzzled me. What debt did I owe? I was just a kid. I was not a perfect angel, but it did not seem to me that I had done anything so horrible that someone needed to die for it.

When I was 12, I watched an episode of the television show *All in the Family* where Edith Bunker was sick. Her minister came to visit and prayed for Edith, saying, "God, please heal this lowly sinner." Archie Bunker, Edith's husband, jumped to his feet, appalled and irate. "How dare you call my wife a sinner!" he railed. "Edith is the sweetest, kindest person alive. She's no sinner!"

I agreed with Archie. I wasn't that bad either. Can't God accept a

---

7   *The Universal Christ* by Richard Rohr, page 15, copyright 2019.

remorseful apology with a vow to do better? Am I so lost and God so bloodthirsty that he needs heads to roll?

I no longer believe a lot of the things I have preached before.

Jesus's death does not, in some macabre, twisted way, convince God to love me, to forgive me, to give me eternal life. Jesus's death was not the payment of a debt to God or the devil. His death did not pacify an angry, bull-headed God who was within a hair of smiting me. Jesus was not a substitute for me in an imaginary celestial courtroom where I am condemned and he takes the death penalty on my behalf. Though such a sacrifice on Jesus's part might make me feel relieved at first, ultimately it makes me feel more miserable and ashamed.

The focus on Jesus's death conveniently pushes the example of his life to the sidelines. "I am saved by the blood," and from having to follow him. The resurrection also becomes superfluous if his death is deemed sufficient.

It took years, but in addition to Jesus dying on the cross, so did my faith in a god who desires and requires suffering and death in order to save the world. However, I do still love to sing many treasured hymns that perpetuate a transactional god.

Jesus died because he threatened the dominating authority of his day. Jesus died because it is our human nature to thrust blame outside of ourselves as a way to resolve a problem. Jesus died because violence is trusted to redeem, set right, clean the slate, and preserve the status quo. No wonder that Christians burned people as heretics and witches, slaughtered Muslims, Jews, and Native Americans, and enslaved, lynched, and abased people of color in the name of Jesus. The slick blood of violence was mistaken for a saintly shine.

At the cross, Jesus does not avoid or eradicate suffering, any more than we can do so in our own lives. At the cross, Jesus the Christ voluntarily joins with us in suffering, shame, victimization, and betrayal, and provides a pathway to healing, hope, and new life. Jesus dies as he lived. No hate or anger or vengeance in the face of the same. He does not respond to evil with more evil. At the cross, Jesus is the Christ unveiling God's heart. He offers forgiveness (as shown to the soldiers), compassion (as given to those crucified with him), and the beloved community (as extended to Mary and the disciple John).

Love is the way Jesus Christ leads, and love invariably involves sacrifice and suffering. We cannot love without loss, whether it is because we forgive, grieve, or give up something that matters to us for a person or principle that matters more. Sacrifice *born from* love and *borne for* love is the most meaningful and joy-producing work of our lives.

The cross does not hang over my head like a sword, demanding that I quiver under its power and show my indebtedness to Jesus. The cross is lifted up from me, along with every expectation to prove myself worthy to be loved.

At the cross, Jesus embodies the divine power of love for me. I am saved because Jesus shows me a way through pain and death. I am saved because the power and presence of Christ on the cross, in some mysterious and wonderful way, bridges all gaps and can make it possible for me to endure, to bear, to overcome. I am saved because Christ lives in me, through me and for me.

Jesus gives me a map that says the world is not flat. I will not fall off the edge, even when I suffer. Even when I die.

C. S. Lewis wrote that God became a human being for the purpose of making us "little Christs."[8] Like Christ the Anointed, we can anoint the world with love that both delights in and doubles down for the good of another. We will suffer. We will also soar.

---

8   *Mere Christianity* by C.S. Lewis, page 200, published in 1952.

(Saint Paul, John Dun Scotus, Reinhold Niebuhr, John McQuarrie, Julian of Norwich, C. S. Lewis, Henri Nouwen, Howard Thurman, Marianne Micks, Renee Girard, Marcus Borg, Walter Brueggemann, Richard Rohr, Barbara Brown Taylor, The Reverend Tom Nicoll and Brian McLaren have shaped my Christology.)

PERICOPE (2012)

I was recently in Arizona for the first time. The visibility of the horizon in every direction is vastly different from our city of trees. Shade is a precious commodity in Arizona. They have to manufacture it. Schools build canopies over playground equipment. Covered parking spaces are a typical perk at apartment complexes. Umbrellas open up on the sunniest of days.

Once when Mormon missionaries rang my bell on a hot July day, I invited them in for a glass of lemonade and an ice cream sandwich. They were both from the West and commented on how the landscape in the East made them feel claustrophobic. The trees blocked their line of sight. I remarked how open fields made me feel undefended. The trees make me feel protected and embraced.

I am reminded of the line in the psalter: "For the Lord God is both sun and shield." (Psalm 84:10) There are times in our life when we need the unobstructed brightness of the sun for its warmth and guidance to encourage us along the way. We are comforted to see where we are headed, our opportunities and challenges clearly visible. But sometimes the sun makes us feel exposed and vulnerable, and we yearn for shade to shelter us as we rest or grieve or think or strengthen our connections with God and loved ones.

I am glad that God is both sun and shield as my needs change, and most of the time I ask God for both at the same time, never sure whether I prefer clarity or coverage for me or those I love. Psalm 84 phrases it better: "For the Lord God is both sun and shield; he will give grace and glory."

CHAPTER 9

WEDDING BAR

I OFFICIATED AT a wedding in Boca Raton, Florida when our daughters were thirteen and eleven. They had never been to a wedding before. The reception was held at a peaches-and-cream colored seaside beach club with a sit-down dinner for two hundred. Everything in the room flowed or fluttered or flowered. My daughters, wide-eyed, took in the ethereal scene. Caroline, the older one, gushed, "This is SO my wedding."

Twenty years later while planning her wedding, I was glad her memory had faded.

Over-the-top weddings were common in Jesus's day. A wedding was considered the happiest day in a person's life. It warranted not just one day of feasting and rejoicing but a full week. A rabbinic law relieved guests at a wedding of any religious observances that might lessen joy. Cheeseburgers for everyone![9] Jesus sets two parables at a wedding, and of course, one of his most famous miracles occurred at a wedding when he turned a lot of water into a lot of wine.

Turning water into wine in order to keep the bar open and the host from any embarrassment seems an odd choice for a holy man. Perhaps it was his starter miracle. He was testing the waters. John is the only gospel writer to tell this story. While I believe there is a great deal of truth — and fact — in John's gospel, he is the hippie of the gospellers. Symbolism and metaphor are his long suit. Did John make up this groovy miracle? Did the other gospel writers not know about it, or did

---

9   Jewish kosher laws prohibit eating dairy products with meat.

they leave it out because they didn't think it was a miracle befitting a Messiah?

I do like how Mary assumes her son will take care of the wine shortage despite his "not now, Mom" response. She doesn't argue with Jesus but tells the servants, "Do whatever he tells you." (John 2:5) She dumps her problem on Jesus, and walks away confident it will be taken care of. Now that preaches.

Many speculate on the wedding's backstory. Some scholars (and novelists) wonder if Jesus himself was the bridegroom, or his sister the bride, which would explain Jesus's mother concern that wine was running out. Baronius, a 16th century priest, submits that once the bridegroom at Cana saw the water miraculously turned into wine, he bade farewell to his bride and followed Jesus, showing to all that celibacy and the apostolate were better than marriage.[10]

From the way couples still line up at the altar, despite Baronius' conclusion or discouraging divorce rates, one might think very little is better than marriage. I say very little is better than a *good* marriage.

Our government also determines marriage to be a good thing and grants married couples several benefits and rights. I remember being taken aback when I first realized that even though I gave birth to her, I was no longer my married daughter's next of kin. Yet I agree that every marriage is not only meant to be wonderful for a couple, but capable of making the world a better place too. When we have someone to come home to, to hold each night, to encourage us and also to rein us in, everyone benefits.

Marriage has revealed to me a way to understand the enigmatic nature of the Trinity. A marriage takes on a life all its own. The soul of the marriage becomes a third person in the relationship. Not only is a couple bonded to one another, but also to the marriage itself. When

---

10   *The Great Commentary of Cornelius A Lapide, translated by Thomas Mossman, 1887, Vol 5.*

my husband gave up on balancing our checkbook, he served not so much me or himself, but the soul of our marriage. When I gave up (almost) being irritated by his tardiness, I served not so much me or him, but the soul of our marriage. A marriage can feed, encourage, inspire, challenge and lift up each person. In the trinity of a marriage, each is distinct and separate but also intricately tied and turned to one another. The soul of the marriage can even continue to live and give after one or both of the couple has grown frail or sick or died.

When I preach at a wedding, I have two critical rules.

1. Brevity. Less than five minutes. Under three, even better. The clock on diminishing returns begins as soon as I start.
2. The target audience is not the bride and groom. It is the married people in the pew.

While I personalize my words for the bridal couple, I know they are not capable of absorbing anything. I shot my wad with them in counseling sessions before the wedding. However, the pews are filled with married couples who likely need to evaluate their contribution to the health of their marriage.

Marriage sets a high bar. Every couple needs to be reminded of just how high and consider if their spouse could say the following: I can rely on you to be kind to me. I can count on you to make choices that honor and protect me, to catch me when I fall, to make sacrifices that lift me up, to be gentle with my hopes and my hurts, to forgive me again and again, to take joy in my joy.

Marriage vows are crazy. Making a promise that is meant to last until parted by death? The only thing crazier is finding someone who wants to make the same promise to you.

When our daughter married, I decided not to serve as the wedding officiant and to be "Mom" only. I was blown away when being Tim's wife at the service eclipsed being Julia Gray's mom.

After Tim "gave" our daughter's hand to her soon-to-be husband, Tim sat down beside me in the pew and took *my* hand. As the wedding proceeded, I became increasingly aware of how our daughter's wedding was also a celebration of our own marriage. Tim and I were flooded with tears of shared joy. I realized that one of the missions of our marriage —to see our children launched and creating their own connections for lifelong love and support—was being fulfilled before our eyes. Look what we have done together! Look what our love has built! I was deeply moved by this unexpected revelation, and I think I would have missed it if I had not been in the pew.

Emotions are intense at weddings. I see bouquets quiver in a bride's trembling hands, and grooms choking on tears. I have presided at a wedding where a bouncer stood on the church steps in case the bride's uninvited father showed up drunk.

Sometimes I begin my wedding homily with humor to relax the couple and the gathered community. When Jim, at age forty-four and after seven years of dating, married Leesa, I opened by saying, "This marriage is very good for my line of work because as a result more people will believe miracles do happen."

When Taylor, the Aussie, married Moore, the Southerner, I welcomed the congregation of two continents by putting vegemite and grits in my accent and offering a hearty "G'day, y'all!"

Second marriages can be more poignant than first ones when they are also proclamations of hope, resurrection and the healing power of love. I referenced the movie, *Pretty Woman*, at a second wedding, saying, "Today I am reminded of the last lines in the less than sacred movie *Pretty Woman*. After Richard Gere climbs the fire escape to reach Julia Roberts, he asks, 'So what happens after he climbs up and rescues her?' and she responds, 'She rescues him right back.' There is a happy redemptive quality to this marriage that is very sacred."

At a wedding where rain poured all day, I remembered what my colleague, The Reverend Patty Rhyne, suggested and collected the day's rain in a bottle. I presented the bottle to the couple, saying:

> This bottle of rainwater is holy water. Use it sparingly because it needs to last seventy years.

> One drop on a furrowed brow has the power to wash away worries and woes.

> Sprinkle in the front yard of every place you live, and peace and joy will grow up around you and in you.

> Pour a little in the fonts of the baptisms of your fifteen children and your babies will sleep all night, and your teenagers will never give you a moment of trouble.

> Mix with love, fidelity and kindness, and your marriage will rain blessings upon you every day.

The joining together of two individuals is called holy matrimony, which brings together two words that, in my book, create an oxymoron. "Holy" means divine and flawless. "Matrimony" is a human endeavor and thereby always flawed. An oxymoron is perfect because nothing reveals better both the human and the holy within us than a marriage does.

We marry because we see the divine in the other. It is what initially and continually draws us to one another. Their warmth, beauty, integrity, kindness, etc. But it will be drawing from the divine within ourselves that will keep us together. Marriages count on our pulling up from our own divine center the God-given grace and love to accept the human and hurting parts of the other, and to persist in believing in his or her greatness and our possibilities together.

I tell couples there are two keys to marital happiness. By the time I meet with a couple, they have already unlocked the first passageway to marital bliss: *Choose your love.* Parents worry about where their child goes to college or what career they choose when they ought to be far more concerned about who their child marries! Who we marry is probably the most important decision we make for our own future happiness, (and it impacts the same for everyone near and dear to us).

The second key is *Love your choice.* If you consistently cherish, listen to, hug, forgive, admire and trust your spouse, then love flourishes for your beloved and flows right back to you.

I visited Helen Wall who at ninety-three, lost her husband of over seven decades. I asked Helen what were her favorite years of being married. She thought for a few seconds and then surprised me saying, "I guess my favorite years were when we were in our seventies. Our children were grown, Jim had retired and we didn't have as many stresses." Wow. I haven't even gotten to the best years of my marriage yet.

Maybe the wedding is the least important part of the story of Jesus changing water into wine, but I have found that marriage *is* a transforming experience. It is intended to improve with age, and if we are lucky, it does have an intoxicating effect.

At the close of a wedding ceremony, I offer this blessing:

> May God who said it is not good be alone, make you one flesh in holy matrimony.

> May Jesus who turned water into wine at a wedding, turn your hearts to one another in fidelity and care.

> And may the Holy Spirit who filled the disciples with boldness, fill your home and life together with joy and love.

Pericope (2015)

My husband gave me a lovely watch for my birthday. I had a basic Timex with big numbers and an indigo light feature for checking the time in the middle of the night or at the movies. It was a bit of a wallflower of a watch, and the one Tim gave me was sleek, classy, and feminine. But it had hashmarks instead of numbers and no indigo light. Tim knew me well enough to say, "I thought it was pretty, but feel free to go back to the store and see if there's a watch you like better."

I went to the jewelry store and was aghast to learn the watch cost twenty times more than my trusty Timex from Walmart. How absurd, I thought. Impractical. We have two kids in college, for goodness' sake. I returned the watch. (Sidebar: I come by this behavior naturally. My mother returned nearly every nice gift my father gave her.)

The next day, my friend Missy Miller asked about my birthday, and I told her about the watch I had returned. Missy looked at me incredulously and said, "Don't be such a ding dong! When your husband does something nice, say 'Thank you!'" Missy is shy that way. I bought my watch back and told Tim "Thank you very much."

Once when Jesus was given an extravagant gift, he was admonished for accepting it. He defended himself by saying that the giver had done a beautiful thing for him. (Matthew 26:6-13) Timeless beauty comes in various forms, and how we receive it differs. We can feel humbled or disconcerted, joyful or dismayed, valued or dismissive. Don't be a ding dong. Gratitude is the door through which we welcome and make room for all manner of loveliness.

CHAPTER 10

LOOSING DEVICES

"EAT YOUR VEGETABLES," Dad used to say to my sisters and me. "It'll put hair on your chest."

We learned early about hyperbole without knowing the word for it.

Jesus is fond of hyperbole and other literary devices. There is irony in the parable of the Good Samaritan and metaphor when Jesus says, "I am the bread of life." (John 6:35) He uses idioms like you "strain out a gnat but swallow a camel." (Matthew 23:24) He makes a pun when he gives the nickname "Peter," meaning "rock," to the disciple who sank in the sea of Galilee but is the pillar of his movement. (Matthew 16:18)

Jesus says many things that need to be read literally and not literally. Most of us understand that when he advises to pluck out our eye or cut off our hand if either causes us to sin, or invites the disciples to eat his flesh and drink his blood, or implies that faith can move mountains, that Jesus's words are not to be read at face value. I do not see many Christians following Jesus's suggestion to "sell what you own and give the money to the poor." (Mark 10:21)

Following Judaic Law gave Jews a distinctive identity that set them apart. For instance, Sabbath keeping was an alien concept to the Gentile world. As the dowager Crawley, played by Maggie Smith, asked on *Downton Abbey*, "What's a weekend?"

Judaic laws about handwashing are now known to be good hygiene, and days of rest to be good for mental and physical health in addition to spiritual wellness, but in ancient times they were trademarks to distinguish Jews from non-Jews, and reflect obedience and honor to God.

Jesus is criticized for healing and working on the Sabbath. He responds by saying, "The Sabbath was made for humankind, not humankind made for the Sabbath." (Mark 2:27) Jesus is a sieve for scripture, sifting to the essential.

Where Jesus is silent in scripture, sometimes words are formulated for him. For instance, Jesus says nothing about homosexuality, yet it is easy to get the impression that his followers heard him say it is an anathema and cause for being rejected and ejected. Jesus did talk about divorce, and for eons his words, read without context, were interpreted to decree that any divorce is shameful and remarriage unacceptable.

In Jesus's day, men could divorce their wives on a whim, and often did, leaving women destitute and stigmatized. Burning dinner was legitimate grounds for divorce. Men married multiple times without personal repercussion. Jesus raises the bar to protect women by making husbands liable for judgment if they remarry and stipulates only one acceptable reason for divorce: unless she is unfaithful, a man cannot divorce his wife. (Matthew19:9) Jesus tightens up the law, the breadth of the husband's commitment and the safeguards to a wife's future. Yet his words were read out of context and twisted to produce horrific and unintended outcomes, especially for women in abusive marriages.

Widows also were preyed upon. Jesus lambasts religious leaders at the temple for "devouring widows' houses." (Mark 12:40) Then right on cue, a widow steps up and drops her last coins in the temple coffer. Jesus says, *Truly I tell you, this poor widow has put in more than all those who are contributing to the treasury. For all of them have contributed out of their abundance; but she out of her poverty has put in everything she had, all she had to live on.* (Mark 12:43-44)

For years I heard Jesus praising the widow for her generosity and faith and sacrifice. She uses the last bit of money she has for a higher purpose. The point of the story seemed clear: be more generous.

Is there another way to interpret Jesus's words? Perhaps Jesus isn't praising the widow at all. Perhaps he is *appalled* at what she is doing. Is this what he meant by devouring widows' houses? Are widows shamed and bullied to give until they have nothing left? Temple scribes routinely took over the care of a widow's estate as she was considered incompetent without a man. The scribes received a percentage of her assets for compensation. Not surprisingly, the practice was notorious for embezzlement and abuse.

Throughout the gospels, Jesus gets more fired up about systemic sin than individual sin. The church has paid more attention to the reverse. Sin that is built in to a government, a religion, or a society to protect those in power and keep those without power broke, is far more egregious and dangerous than the failings of one person.

Another way to read today's gospel story is to hear Jesus, saying, *Look at this woman! Here is another example of a widow you have intimidated and preyed upon and left destitute.*

Jesus has no patience for oppressive behavior, particularly when it masquerades as piety. For example, ritual purity in first-century Palestine was expensive. The food you ate, the dishes you used, the cleanliness of your hands and feet meant that strict adherence to the rules was feasible only for people of means. Pharisees had resources and time to enact ritual purity. The poor did not and were often labeled as outcasts, unclean, and unworthy.

Jesus harshest words are for the religious elite who are consumed with what goes into their mouths but not what comes out. What comes out of Jesus's mouth about them is unequivocal and explicit.

Snakes! Brood of vipers! Hypocrites! Blind guides! Fools! Whitewashed tombs ... full of all kinds of filth! (Matthew 23:13,17, 27, 33)

Jesus's beef with the Pharisees is that their holiness comes at the expense of other people. The traditions accomplished the opposite of what they were intended to do: they overshadowed, even canceled out, the inward cultivation of piety and faith. They cut off access to community and human flourishing. The Pharisees' interpretation of holy writings hurt people, and made God look like a schmuck.

Jesus aligns himself with the prophets who declared that any spiritual ritual or practice that does not lead to kindness, mercy, or justice is not only empty and useless but abhorrent to God.

Whenever we read scripture, we undergo the task of interpreting what we read. All scripture is read through the lens of personal experience. The rabbis of Jesus's day and in the centuries before Jesus did what is called "loosing and binding." Rabbis applied the Torah to daily practical issues, loosening the grip of some rules and tightening or extending others. Jesus does the same thing. For instance, he binds murder to anger, and adultery to lust. He extends the commandment on loving neighbors to include loving enemies. But he looses Sabbath-keeping laws so that one can harvest grain and heal on the Sabbath. The Sermon on the Mount is an example of Jesus binding and loosing Judaic Law to guide us, to free us, to compel us, to draw us into deeper and more meaningful community with God and with one another.

Jewish rituals and practices nose their way into the nooks and crannies of daily life. Not just what to eat but how to prepare food, and which foods are eaten, or not eaten, together. Not just washing up, but how and when and what to wash. Rules cover worship but also marriage, sex, parenting, shopping, clothing, and running a business. Pharisees, often painted only as bad guys, were largely responsible for sustaining Jewish identity and community.

Jewish laws seek a complete integration of body and soul, of the holy and the ordinary. Set apart but no separation between who one is and how one lives. This is not hyperbole. Ambitious, yes, and also life-giving.

When Jesus says pluck out your eye or cut off a hand that causes you to sin, he exaggerates to emphasize how critical it is to cut anything out of our life that leads away from God and God's ways, but not because we have become unacceptable to God. Rather, in a twist of irony, our pursuit of perfection cuts us off from experiencing and sharing the grace and generosity of God.

My sisters and I gathered to help our parents cull through items stored in the large basement of their home of forty-five years. Rusty appliances, faded magazines, dated clothing, chipped vases. A bag of colored aquarium rocks. Burger King paper crowns. An Easy-Bake Oven.

As we deemed what was unusable, unwanted, and ready for the dump, our mother grew testy, anxious, and defensive. We needed to review our goal. To clean out the basement or to help our parents? Our process disrespected them. We were not helping. We were hurting.

We changed course. We asked for the stories and meaning behind stored items. We lingered over photographs. We showed appreciation for the souvenirs of our childhood. It was not the paper crowns that needed to go, but our insensitivity, our "git er done" business mode.

Loosing and binding priorities, goals, rules, and regulations is challenging, dangerous, and necessary. Being an avenue for the healing work and power of God's love is the primary rule, and anything that gets in the way needs to be plucked and pitched.

PERICOPE (2021)

My dad was a high school English teacher. He was home by 4:30 P.M. which was a boon for me and my sisters. He didn't travel and had dinner with us every night. Except on Wednesdays when he played volleyball and ate at the Y. On those nights, Mom took a break and opened a can of Chef Boyardee Beefaroni for our dinner.

Dad was home all summer. He played gin rummy and tennis with us. My little sister, Ginny, earned a shoe box of blue ribbons on swim team with Dad cheering the loudest back when swim meets were in the middle of weekdays and most dads couldn't attend. When others asked what he was doing for the summer, Dad would say he was "on sabbatical." That was the first time I heard that word.

As a priest, my parish has given me the gift of a sabbatical more than once. Of course, the word has biblical roots. Keeping the Sabbath day holy is the fifth commandment, but before Moses received all ten, God instructed the Israelites in the wilderness to rest on the Sabbath. Honoring the Sabbath is really the first commandment God issued. Perhaps because the others can't be kept if this one isn't.

Rabbi Jonathan Sacks points out that on the Sabbath, "all hierarchies of power are suspended. There are no masters and slaves, employers and employees. Even domestic animals cannot be made to work… We are not allowed to exercise control over another form of life or even forces of nature…all are free and all are equal."[11] Sacks says the Sabbath gives us the chance to practice living in utopia.

It makes sense, therefore, that studies show teachers have the least difficulty adjusting to retirement. They get to practice in the summers.*

---

11   *Covenant and Conversation by Jonathan Sacks, page 17, copyright 2010*

Take a sabbatical from all the things you do to prove or improve yourself. Practice watching the sun rise or set. Play. Plant. Putter. Lay down the scorecard. Lay yourself down. Splash. Sprawl. Spectate. Open a can of Chef Boyardee for supper.

*Unless of course, they have to find other means of income because of abysmal teacher pay.

CHAPTER 11

THE YOUNG AND THE RESTLESS

WHEN I WAS growing up, my favorite cartoons and television programs included a child. I preferred the *Flintstones* episodes with Pebbles or Bamm-Bamm. I liked the *Andy Griffith Shows* that revolved around Opie best. And, showing my age, I adored the *Little Rascals* with Spanky, Alfalfa, and all the gang. Bible stories with children appealed to me as well. Moses in the bulrushes. David outsmarting Goliath. Jesus going to the temple as a boy. And the horrifying but absorbing story of King Solomon threatening to cut a baby in half to determine the child's true mother might be my all-time favorite.

The bible tells us that Jesus had brothers and sisters. (Mark 3:32) It is very likely he was "'Uncle Jesus" to a full house of nieces and nephews. There are recorded occasions of Jesus engaging with children. Children were likely at the River Jordan with their parents who were getting dunked, and at the wedding in Cana with their parents who were getting drunk. The bible records the presence of children at the feeding of the five thousand, and they probably fidgeted through the Sermon on the Mount. Children play a central role in five of Jesus's parables. The gospels tell four stories in which Jesus heals a child, and of the three people Jesus raises from the dead, two are children. After Jesus overturns the moneychangers' tables in the temple, Matthew's gospel tells us that the children in the temple, not the adults, shout "'Hosanna' to the Son of David." A child was likely present at the Last Supper to ask the opening four questions that begin a seder meal. A well-known and oft-painted scene from Jesus's life is when he invites babies and children to his side, cradles them in his arms, and blesses them—all to the dismay and confusion of his disciples.

In Matthew's gospel, we are told Jesus makes his home in Capernaum and is there when his disciples ask who is the greatest in the kingdom of heaven. Jesus beckons a child to his side and says "unless you change and become like children," greatness in the kingdom will evade you. (Matthew 18:3)

I wonder who the child is. One of his nieces or nephews? The son, daughter, or younger sibling of one of the disciples? A neighbor's child? Several books of fiction imagine that Jesus was married or had a child. That possibility intrigues me without unraveling who Jesus is for me. If he did not have a child of his own, I am glad, for Jesus's sake, that he had children in his life.

Though stories with children caught my eye when I was a child, now I wish there were more stories about Jesus and old people. Better yet—I want to know old Jesus. Gray-haired Jesus. Hard-of-hearing Jesus. Miralax Jesus. Babies have a universal appeal, and the baby Jesus has been a part of my spiritual connection to God. Retired Jesus could inspire me now.

The life expectancy in Jesus's day was dragged down by a high infant and child mortality rate. Those who survived to ten years old had a chance to live into their sixties or even eighties. But no story in the gospel specifically describes an encounter between an elderly person and the adult Jesus. Jesus heals a woman stooped over with a bad back. Perhaps old age bent her back, but she could have been born that way. Jesus heals a man lying by the pool of Siloam who is said to have been an invalid for thirty-eight years. He might have been a senior citizen, but again, it is not clear.

When Jesus tells Nicodemus that "unless he is born again he cannot see the kingdom of God," Nicodemus counters with a great question. "How can anyone be born after having grown old?" (John 3:4)

Yes! Now that I am past sixty this question has new meaning for me. As I age, I hope the best is not all behind me. I don't want to rest on my laurels and settle for second rate for the rest of my life. I want to stir my imagination with perspectives and possibilities I have never considered. I want to expect unexpected joys that release an inner light and lightness in me. I want to wield my wisdom and history to bless others.

Aging makes me more attuned to feelings and experiences and relationships that transcend my stiff joints and mental lapses. While my death grows nearer and more real, births come closer and dearer. I see the continuum of which I am a part. I am not slowly moving toward a steep cliff that ends it all. My death, like my birth, is a part of a steady, endless stream that keeps joining something larger and deeper.

The gospel of Luke tells of two people who meet the infant Jesus, and their advanced age is the story's poignant hinge.

Anna and Simeon are revered by the Jewish community. Anna, at eighty-four, is called a prophetess, and Simeon has a revelation that he will not see death until his eyes see Christ. These two leathery faces peer at a silky newborn, and something new is born within them.

A few days before ninety-seven-year-old Juanita Neas died, she met her new great-granddaughter, Emeline. I saw a photo of their meeting. Baby Emeline's mouth is open in laughter. She is bright as a new penny. Juanita gazes at Emeline. Her face is pure contentment. She appears pleased, relieved, to pass on the baton, to pass on the love and grace that has been hers and is now Emeline's. To live long enough to delight in a great-grandchild is a supreme blessing.

Jesus never has wrinkly skin that bruises with the slightest tap. His torso never resembles a melting ice cream cone. He doesn't tell stories of grandfathers or grandmothers or mention anything about growing old. He is more subtle. Old people don't recognize themselves (ourselves) in mirrors anyway. So Jesus tells a parable about a man who dies suddenly with his barns full of wealth that he can't take along with him, and a parable about a mean man who dies and can't take back the mean things he did. Jesus advises not to treasure what can be ruined by rust and moth.

He talks about old wineskins. (Luke 5:37) Animal skins were common containers for wine. They were lighter to carry and less likely to break than pottery. The elasticity of new wineskins allowed them to stretch and expand when new wine continued to ferment and emit gases. Old wineskins stiffened and lost pliancy. Old wineskins burst holding new wine. They couldn't hack it.

So maybe Jesus does know about aging. If I want new ideas, new relationships, new purpose, new usefulness, I cannot be an old *whine*skin. With age, I have the advantage of the long view on situations, and can see that being less easily offended and more generous of heart and mind teaches resilience and promotes understanding. As my father's daughter, it is all I can do to keep from correcting people's grammar. Millennials have trouble with pronouns. I want to burst when I hear "Him and I went to the store." I need to connect instead of correct.

Betty Pledger was in her nineties and living in a nursing home. She was one of the first women to receive a Burger King franchise, and she built an empire with a hard-ass reputation. We sat on a bench outside her nursing home. Her heart was giving out. She could not drive or read and needed help to walk, but she told me she still had one thing she could do. "I can compliment people," she said. People age but they can also grow. Her heart *was* giving out.

When Jesus turned water into wine at the wedding in Cana, the guests complimented the host for saving the best wine for last. I know that aging is not easy, but it can be savored. My three-month-old grandson, Sam, sat attentively in my lap as I read a book that illustrated the lyrics from "What a Wonderful World." I crooned "I hear babies cry. I watch them grow. They'll learn much more than I'll ever know," and the wonder of the world tasted very sweet *because* of my age.[12]

---

12   *What a Wonderful World*, lyrics by Bob Thiele and George David Weiss, 1967

Pericope (2021)

I took my two-year-old great-niece, Joyce, to the Lazy 5 Ranch on a dreary, overcast day. Afterward we enjoyed some ice cream. She was wearing a coat, but I wasn't, and when I shivered and said "Brrr," Joyce started pulling her jacket off and asked, "You want my coat?"

I repeat: she was two.

A study done in 2018, determined that how empathetic we are is partly due to our genes.[13] Though only a small percentage of us are born with an innate capacity for empathy. Most of us have to be taught.

Perhaps teaching empathy is one of the church's most important roles. If we are to love our neighbor as ourselves, we have to listen to our neighbor. We have to know what our neighbor needs. We have to be willing to not just feel *for* our neighbor but feel *with* them. Empathy doesn't require agreeing with someone but appreciating what someone is experiencing. As Brené Brown says, empathy is communicating the healing message: "You are not alone."[14] Turns out that 100% of us thrive on that sort of human connection and belonging.

Empathy connects us, even when we think we are polar opposites.

Jesus taught empathy when he told parables like the Good Samaritan, the Workers in the Vineyard, and the Lost Sheep. He challenged us to remove the plank from our own eye before we get our panties in a wad about the splinter in our neighbor's eye. Jesus modeled empathy by the people he embraced and engaged. His own inner circle included

---

13   "Study finds that Genes Play a Role in Empathy" by Matheus Ferrero on University of Cambridge website, March 2018.

14   *Daring Greatly: How the Courage to be Vulnerable Transforms the Way We Live, Love, Parent and Lead* by Brene Brown, page 81, copyright 2012.

a revolutionary and a reactionary. Jesus crossed the aisle on a regular basis. His life became the aisle where people were seen, heard, valued, healed, and united.

Empathy yields kindness. It is what gives us courage to stand up to a bully whether we are the victim or the bystander. Empathy builds stronger relationships by increasing trust, support, and happiness. Empathy is key to effective leadership and human flourishing. As Theodore Roosevelt is quoted as saying, "No one cares how much you know until they know how much you care."

If you are like my great-niece, Joyce, empathy is easy for you. If you are like me and the overwhelming majority of us, empathy must be learned and practiced *ad nauseum* until it becomes *au natural*.

CHAPTER 12

POWER SHIFT

ONE OF THE most effective and crushing things my mother said to me when I was growing up was "You are getting too big for your britches." This meant Mom thought I was thinking more highly of myself than I deserved to think, or I was acting spoiled. For my mother, the parable Jesus tells about a man who presumptively takes a primo seat at a dinner party table and then is asked to move to a lower position is exactly the cautionary tale she preached.

I felt out of my league at a formal dinner where everyone at the table was either a current or retired justice on the North Carolina Supreme Court. Seated next to me was the chief justice. I tried to channel everything I'd learned watching episodes of *Matlock* and *Law and Order*. What could I possibly say that he and I might share in common? "Oh, hey, I wear a robe at work too!"?

As the chief justice and I chatted, I learned that he was in the throes of raising teenagers. Bingo. There is nothing like parenting teens to level the playing field. The chief justice might have wielded great authority and power from the highest court in our state, but I knew he was as hapless as anyone at raising teenagers.

Jesus says, "The exalted will be humbled and the humble will be exalted." Depending upon one's circumstances, this comes across as either a threat or a hope. Yet is flipping the world's fortunes all Jesus meant to convey?

When I graduated from high school I worked at a Christian-sponsored camp in Colorado on what was called the work crew. The work crew did not get paid. Thirty of us came from around the country to serve. We did not know what job we would be assigned until we arrived. The popular jobs were to work with the horses, or to be a waiter in the dining hall, or to work the mailroom and deliver campers' letters. Two boys and two girls were given the task of cleaning bathrooms. Guess what job I got? As an indication of how privileged my childhood was, when I told my mother about my assignment, she laughed and said, "You've gone across the country to clean a toilet for the first time."

I shared the job with a girl from Minnesota. We made up songs about our work and wielded our plunger and brushes like majorette batons. At the end of the season, two members of our work crew were invited to address the entire camp—comprising some 300 teenagers—about why our faith had brought us to camp to serve. I was one of the two who were chosen. It was my first experience of talking about my faith before a group of people. I had been humbled by my job cleaning bathrooms, and now I was exalted to speak. This happened five years before it entered my head to become a priest, but I knew that I was meant for that moment. And to be so honored and elevated also deeply humbled me.

I experience this phenomenon often in ministry. One of the most humbling privileges of officiating at a funeral, or leading a support group, or walking into a hospital room, is to be permitted into someone's life at a vulnerable moment. People look to me for help and guidance. I might be able to offer comfort, strength, or hope, but I could unintentionally deepen their pain—and that makes me feel vulnerable too.

A certain amount of confidence and hubris is required to climb into a pulpit, to pick up a scalpel, to fly an airplane, to advocate in court, to shepherd a roomful of students, or to run for political office. Yet if the experience of exaltation, of being given authority, responsibility, and privilege, does not also humble us, then we are either headed for disaster, or disaster will come to those in our wake.

The humbling of the exalted is not designed to punish, but to save us from ourselves. Humility promotes self-awareness and empathy in ways that success cannot teach. Humility can increase effectiveness and prepare a person for more responsibility. Those who remain exalted become uncoachable and stop growing.

Ashley Merryman co-author of *NurtureShock,* asserts that humility emboldens people to aspire to their highest potential. People who have the faith and courage to admit they need help, and know they can benefit from the expertise and experience of others who have less power, are the ones who end up with greater gains.[15]

An example of humbling and exalting is the story of Jesus healing a woman while on his way to help someone else. (Luke 8:40-56)

The story begins with Jesus arriving by boat to a town on the edge of the Sea of Galilee. A crowd quickly gathers. Rumors about Jesus make folks curious, and eager to hear Jesus speak or perform a miracle. A man named Jairus, a leader in the local synagogue, begs Jesus to come to his house and heal his sick twelve-year-old daughter. Jesus goes with him.

On his way to heal the child, who has likely lived a of life of relative privilege and plenty all of her twelve years, Jesus stops to help a woman who has lived a life of pain and persecution for the same twelve years. The woman lost all her money on doctors. She has a constant hemorrhage, most likely a gynecological condition. It is horrifying to consider what sort of medical procedures she might have endured. The flow of blood makes her a pariah, untouchable and banned from homes, the market, and the synagogue. She does not presume to ask Jesus for help. Touching her would make Jesus unclean. Hoping to go undetected, she reaches out her hand to graze the hem of his garment, confident that the slightest brush with what Jesus is wearing can heal her.

---

15   *Leaders* Are *More Powerful When They are Humble, New Research Shows,* by Ashley Merriman, article in The Washington Post, December 8, 2016

Meanwhile, a crowd surrounds Jesus on his way to Jairus's house, hoping to witness a miracle. When Jesus stops and asks, "Who touched me?" his disciples are puzzled. People press on him from every side.

What follows is a lovely encounter between Jesus and a woman who has not been listened to or treated with respect or dignity in more than a decade.

For even longer, I was oblivious to another lovely lesson embedded in the story.

Notice what Jairus, the influential, desperate father does. Or what he doesn't do. He waits. He does not object when Jesus stops the progression to his sick daughter's bedside. He does not point out that the woman with the hemorrhage is less important than his child. He waits.

We witness a shift in power. It moves from Jairus, near the top of the social ladder, to a woman at the bottom rung. Jairus lays down his privilege at great personal cost. He shares his power with the least privileged person in his community. No wonder he is the respected leader of the synagogue. For years, I missed one of the most inspiring messages in this story. Jesus reveals divine power as shareable power.

As a white, college-educated, employed, property-owning, debt-free United States citizen, I know far more about an exalted life than a humbled one. Jesus's nonviolent and seemingly acquiescent approach to oppression must disappoint many who do not enjoy the social and financial capital that I do. Armed resistance at least feels like one is doing something to create change.

In Howard Thurman's 1949 classic, *Jesus and the Disinherited*, he writes, "Jesus recognized that … anyone who permits another to determine the quality of his inner life gives into the hands of the other the keys to his destiny."[16] When others know what can make us lose our temper or

---

16   *Jesus and the Disinherited* by Howard Thurman, page 18, published in 1949.

equilibrium, Thurman says, they can keep us under subjection.

Jesus does not desire to swap the possession of power but to make it accessible and beneficial to all. Taking or redistributing power by force still calls for oppressive behavior. Doing so by choice calls for compassion and a desire to understand one another.

Jesus's life, from beginning to end, brings the exalted and humbled together. At his birth, both blue-collar shepherds and wealthy astronomers kneel at the manger. Among Jesus's closest followers are poor fishermen. Roman collaborators and women of means bankroll his ministry. He welcomes a prostitute to a rich man's dinner party. At the crucifixion, when it appears that Jesus is stripped of all power, the condemned man becomes the most powerful person in the room when he forgives his executioners. At his death, the wealthy Joseph of Arimathea and Jesus's own poor mother take down his body and place it in the tomb, while a Roman officer declares him divine.

Throughout the Hebrew scriptures, the sharing of power is also taught and modeled, from the genesis of God's image shared between male and female, to the freeing of the Israelites from slavery, to the prophet's clarion call for justice to roll down like an ever-flowing stream.

Shareable power is also modeled in the trinity. No one person of the trinity is more powerful than another.

The humble are exalted and the exalted are humbled. This is not an either/or. It is the pattern of growth and transformation. It is the ebb and flow of all creation. Watch the ocean tides or the moon wax and wane. As Samuel Wells and Marcia Owen wrote in their book *Living without Enemies*, "Receiving God's love is like breathing in. Responding to the suffering of others is like breathing out. If I do the first without the second, I will pass out."[17]

---

17   *Living Without Enemies: Being Present in the Midst of Violence* by Samuel Wells and Marcia Owen, page 134, copyright 2011.

Humility can lead to greatness, and true greatness always calls us back to humility. It is the way of Jesus and the path of our transformation to becoming our finest and authentic selves.

Pericope (2015)

Timothy Shriver grew up helping his mom organize athletic games and activities in their backyard for people with physical and intellectual challenges. His mother, Eunice Shriver, founded the Special Olympics, and Timothy is its executive director. I heard him speak at a conference.

Watching an organization grow from the beginning, Shriver felt he was well qualified to serve as its quarterback and knew where the goalposts were. Then he had an epiphany that changed the playing field for him, uncovering the true mission of the Special Olympics.

Loretta Claiborne completed more than twenty-five marathons in the Special Olympics. Her best time was three hours and three minutes. Shriver saw her as their perfect spokesperson. Her life proved that, despite her poor eyesight and intellectual disability, she was smart and gifted enough to succeed.

Shriver heard Claiborne speak and expected her to talk about how she belonged in the real world, but her words caught him off guard.

Claiborne said, "Come into my world...In my world, we don't have any enemies...in my world, we don't look at what a person can't do... everyone has a chance to belong and there's nobody who gets rejected or left out or excluded. [Our world is] strong and joyful and you can't beat that."[18]

For Shriver, it was a transformative moment. "All my life, I had wanted to help people like Loretta join my world," he said. "I realized I needed to be more like her and join their world."[19]

---

18   *Fully Alive* by Timothy Shriver, page, 138, copyright 2014.
19   From presentation given at Center for Contemplation and Action Conspire Conference in Albuquerque, New Mexico, July 15 2015.

Christianity can come off as an organization that is trying to help us fit into heaven. We are misfits who better up our game if we want to belong in the next world. But Jesus invites us, as we are, to join his world where there are no scorecards or battlegrounds, where there is more joy over one lost lamb found than for ninety-nine who never stray. Turns out heaven is run by a misfit.

CHAPTER 13

THE EYE DOCTOR

MY HUSBAND IS an ophthalmologist. Tim's bread-and-butter surgery is uncrossing eyes, especially for children. Jesus is also concerned about vision.

The entire nineth chapter of John's gospel recounts the story of a blind man receiving sight. As is typical of John, the story is rife with irony and imagery. Jesus proclaims he is the light of the world and then brings light into a blind man's world. The blind man recognizes Jesus's divinity faster than those who have their sight. Paralleling the Genesis creation, Jesus scoops clay from the ground onto the man's eyes to create his vision. The story ends with Jesus's cross-eyed declaration that he has come to bring sight to the blind, and to blind those who can see.

The Pharisees in the story are highly skeptical that Jesus healed a man who was born blind. As the gospel points out, "Never since the world began has it been heard that anyone opened the eyes of a person born blind." (John 9:32)

The Pharisees might have been familiar with sight being restored to people whose blindness developed with age. Cataract surgery, using a proverbial stick in the eye, was first mentioned as early as 1750 BC in the Hammurabi Code. Not only is the surgery described, the Code also outlines a payment plan for the services, which includes the removal of the surgeon's fingers if things do not go well.

My husband, who still has all ten of his fingers, explained to me why it is miraculous for an adult who is born blind to be able to see. The brain of a baby born blind does not receive pictures and images from the eyes. When no pictures—or only fuzzy, dim ones—are received for several years, the brain never learns how to process the film it is given from the eyes, how to make a clear picture into clear vision. Even if the eyes become healthy later, by the time a child is ten years old, the brain has lost its capacity to learn how to process a clear picture.

The Pharisees refuse to believe the man's story. They interview his parents to verify his blindness since birth. They grill the once-blind man to confess that he is an accomplice to a hoax and that the alleged healer is a sinner. The man claims he does not even know the name of his miracle worker, but says, "If this man were not from God, he could do nothing." (John 9:33)

Restoring vision, opening eyes, and helping people process what they see in new ways is central to Jesus's and the church's mission.

There is an app for the blind and colorblind called Color Identifier. Place your phone camera over anything and it tells you what color it is—very helpful when deciding what to wear. A woman who lost her sight as an adult wrote about how the app has worked for her in unexpected ways. Not only does it help her match pants and shirts, it has influenced her outlook on life. The app does not just identify blue or yellow, but is far more specific. Her yard is not green, but Avocado, Rangoon Green, or Asparagus. Blue is Cornflower, Wedgewood, Cobalt, and Sapphire. The sky might be Baltic Sea on a bright day and Gunsmoke on a cloudy day. Her office is not beige but Nutmeg, Bamboo, Oregano, Mustard, and Potter's Clay. When she went to see her father in the gloom and gray at the ICU, her app saw Evening Fog, Silver Teapot, and Castle Gate. As she wrote, what we choose to see colors our perspective.[20]

Jesus says he came to give the blind sight and to make the seeing blind. Perhaps he means that sometimes the sighted need to be blinded in order to see with the heart instead of the eyes.

---

20   I was unable to find where I first read this story.

The spiritual journey can be understood as the movement from seeing God nowhere or only where we expect to see him, to seeing God everywhere, and especially where we least expect.

Years ago, I stitched a bible verse to hang in Tim's office. Matthew 6:22. "The eye is the lamp of the body. So if your eye is sound, your whole body will be full of light."

At President Biden's inauguration, Amanda Gorman brought us to our feet and tears to our eyes with her poetry, closing with these lines: "For there is always light, if only we are brave enough to see it / If only we are brave enough to be it."[21] Her words echo Matthew 6:22.

This has become my favorite bible verse. It covers wildflower-covered meadows of spiritual territory. Not only is it a beautiful description of how Tim's and my professions overlap, it encapsulates Jesus's teaching.

Seeing is not believing. Believing is seeing. What we believe determines what we can see and who we can be. If we believe that love is stronger than hate, that there is a way forward from an impasse, that hope lives beyond loss, then we can also see it and we too will become the light of the world.

---

21   "The Hill We Climb" by Amanda Gorman, copyright 2021.

Pericope (2021)

Recently I enjoyed the best tasting pancakes I have ever eaten. No berries or whipped cream. Not even butter.

They were fluffy, flavorful, and they filled me with hope.

When the unadorned, mundane stuff of life is elevated and experienced with new appreciation and unexpected delight, I am reminded that I don't need the most updated, uploaded and upgraded in order to be uplifted.

Jesus pointed to common objects and occupations to reveal uncommon and life-giving wisdom. Seeds, birds and bread became examples of faith, peace of mind and grace. He told stories where working class trades of baking, fishing and shepherding contained the essence of greatness, leadership and mercy.

Hope is not manufactured by the extraordinary and the exceptional. The smell of brewing coffee, a soft kiss, soup stirred on the stove, a stranger's smile, a handwritten letter, the song of crickets, a warm word, a baby's laugh, a hand reaching out for yours, something lost found, a hammer's task, the moon's glow and star shine can all convey the presence of beauty, kindness, caring, love and trust which are the building blocks of hope.

I didn't think it was possible for something as common and simple as a stack of pancakes to take it up a notch and surprise me. I think buttermilk was involved.

CHAPTER 14

JOHN 3:16 UNHINGED

I WAG MY finger. It's my yellow highlighter and indicates that I'm saying something I want to remember or emphasize. My husband, always the helpful one, alerts me to when my wagging finger comes out by wagging his finger right back at me. I think he is fortunate that my vice doesn't involve a different finger.

Some bibles highlight Jesus's words by printing them in red letters. The most well-known red-lettered words are from John 3:16.

Rollen Stewart, donning a rainbow-colored wig, became famous for waving a John 3:16 placard at major sporting events from the late 1970s to the 1990s. The television cameras found him at the Super Bowl, the NBA Finals, the Olympics, the Kentucky Derby, and a surprise appearance at the wedding of Lady Diana and Prince Charles. No doubt Stewart inspired many people to look up the bible verse. He also made John 3:16 the butt of a joke, and he the de facto spokesperson for Christianity. John 3:16 became the bible's version of both a wagging finger and a middle finger to the world.

The verse sounds innocent enough. "For God so loved the world that he gave his only Son, so that everyone who believes in him may not perish but may have eternal life."

Stewart, and many before him and since, have used the verse as a formula for salvation, a litmus test for who is in and who is out. Believe in Jesus, and you're good to have eternal life. Don't believe and you're damned. It's as simple as liking someone on Facebook or Instagram. Save yourself before it is too late and "like" Jesus.

When our children were young, my husband read them a story from a children's bible at bedtime. The theology in the children's bible could unhinge me so it worked better if Tim read from it. The version of the parable of the lost sheep drove me crazy. It ended with this moralizing: when a person turns away from sin and comes back to God, God is very, very happy. I got incensed because nowhere in the parable does the lost lamb say "I'm sorry" or even recognize it is lost, or turn back. And that seemed to me to be the point of the story!

Rick Morley, an Episcopal priest, wrote a book called *Going to Hell, Getting Saved, and What Jesus Actually Says.* Morley studied everything that Jesus said about salvation in the gospels. He was shocked to discover that the gospel of Mark says absolutely nothing that links salvation to faith or repentance or saying a little prayer. Matthew and Luke, the same. Eternal life is tied to loving one's neighbor, visiting the sick, feeding the hungry, giving up possessions, being like a child. Nothing about faith or saying any formulaic confession of belief as the linchpin to salvation. What became clear to Morley is that Jesus did not give one official line on the pathway to salvation.[22]

Yet folks waving John 3:16 signs suggest otherwise. Those sign wavers may be genuinely concerned about me and how and where I will spend eternity, but they give the impression that *they* are more concerned about me than *God* is. God's love has an expiration date on it. If I die without uttering words of faith, his love for me will go sour.

I want to wave another sign, one bringing attention to John 6:39: "And this is the will of him who sent me, that I should lose nothing of all that he has given me, but raise it up on the last day."

Looking at the totality and breadth of Jesus's life and ministry and teaching, I see a wide mercy and a relentless love. Jesus is far more concerned that we be Christlike than that we like Christ. Somehow

---

22   *Going to Hell, Getting Saved and What Jesus Actually Said,* by Rick Morley, copyright 2011

over the years, we made the very inclusive Jesus the head of a very exclusive movement.

Mahatma Gandhi was a Hindu and one of the greatest followers of Jesus's teaching in the last one hundred years. Gandhi said, "I like your Christ, I do not like your Christians. Your Christians are so unlike your Christ." Case in point: rainbow-wigged Stewart is serving three lifetime sentences for kidnapping

Christianity does not have a corner on the market. God is available and accessible everywhere. Creation is the first bible, the first revelation, the first time that God shows God's face. As Paul writes: "Ever since God created the world, God's everlasting power and divinity, however invisible, has been there for the mind to see in the things God has made." (Romans 1:20)

Missionaries who spread and model Jesus's message of grace, compassion, and justice, who support resistance to evil and abusive power, who collaborate to build communities of equity, healing, and love, have my utmost respect. I do not believe that the purpose of missionary work is to save people from eternal damnation, but to expose people who do not know Jesus to his way, truth, and life—and to reveal to those who do know Jesus how God is already present and perceptible long before the gospel arrived. It is a mutual conversion experience.

Franciscan priest Richard Rohr was a young deacon on a Navajo reservation when he noticed a mother and her children engaging in a ritual each morning at sunrise on their doorstep. "She and the children would be reaching out with both hands uplifted to 'scoop' up the new day and then 'pour' it over their heads and bodies as if in a blessing. I would sit in my truck until they were finished, thinking how silly it was of us Franciscans to think *we* brought religion to New Mexico four hundred years ago."[23]

---

23   Adapted from Richard Rohr, an unpublished talk, February 2018, St. John XXIII Catholic Community, Albuquerque, New Mexico.

God loves all that God creates, and God's love for us is far more obvious, splashy, and flamboyant than a man wearing a multi-colored wig and holding a sign. If we want nothing to do with light, hope, and peace—no matter our theology—God respects that desire on our part, and we can choose a life free from those ideals. We call that hell, whether we experience it now or later. But I believe that hell is always temporary. God's love is eternally irrepressible and irresistible. It never leaves the table. As my colleague the Reverend Chip Edens said, "God's power to love us is greater than our power to reject God."

At the resurrection, we see that death is not a hard stop. It is a threshold. It is a crossover point but not a cross-off point, because ... God so loved us.

Pericope (2018)

Can polar opposites find common ground?

A friend recently published a book. He is a doctor who retired a few years ago after being diagnosed with cancer. Michael Rotberg is Jewish, and we have always appreciated each other's strong interest in spiritual matters.

In his book, *Practice: Becoming a Better Doctor, Patient, and Person,* Michael tells the story of a camp counselor at a Christian camp who invited campers to stand in a circle around a campfire. He told them to point at the fire and then asked, "Where are you pointing?"

"At the fire, of course," they replied.

"Right," he went on, "you are all pointing at the fire, but look. Sally is pointing north. Bill is pointing east. Jeremy is pointing south. Everyone is pointing in a different direction, but you are all pointing at the same thing."[24]

The counselor showed that where we stand, what we see from our vantage point, will determine the direction we point. Someone who appears to be pointing in the polar opposite direction as we are could actually be pointing at the same thing and want to be warmed by the same fire.

I think this campfire metaphor is handy and helpful whether discussing religion, politics, or what color to paint the living room. The bible talks more about holy ground than common ground, but the latter is always

---

[24]   *Practice: Becoming a Better, Doctor, Patient and Person* by Michael Rotberg, pages 189-190, copyright 2018.

sacred space when we realize, though poles apart, that our hearts are in the same place.

P.S. Michael Rotberg died of cancer at sixty-four in 2019. At his funeral, two of his friends, a rabbi and a Baptist minister, gave eulogies.

CHAPTER 15

PRAYER ART

I met with a couple in preparation for marriage and discovered a significant difference of opinion between them.

The bride said "I love you" multiple times a day—at the end of the day, at every parting during the day, and at the close of every phone conversation. If she forgot to say it, she would call her fiancé back. The groom, on the other hand, thought that saying it too often diluted its meaning. Watered it down. I asked him how often he thought it was appropriate to say he loved her. He thought for a moment. "About twice a month," he said.

The Lord's Prayer can lose its meaning by overuse. Most Christians memorize it and go on autopilot when saying it. Every service in our Episcopal Book of Common Prayer includes an instruction to say the Lord's Prayer, calling for it to be prayed thirty-eight different times.

When my father was weeks from death, his priest visited him. Dad had dementia with profound short-term memory loss, but much of his personality remained intact. As his priest was about to leave, he asked Dad if he remembered how to say the Lord's Prayer. Dad looked at him, smiled, and whispered, "I can say it backwards."

The disciples asked Jesus how to pray. Someone took notes, and Jesus's response became the signature prayer for Christians. Yet it is interesting to note that the prayer is ecumenical. There is no mention of Jesus. The prayer is suited for anyone who believes in a higher power. It begins with "Our," a pronoun that indicates there is only one family.

The Lord's Prayer uncovers something about Jesus's relationship with Joseph. Jesus chooses to call God "Father" not because God was his literal father. God did not beget Jesus. Fatherhood is the closest human relationship that Jesus chooses to compare to his relationship to God.

For some, calling God "Father" is an obstacle. Their experiences are not like those that Jesus might have had with Joseph. A prison chaplain tells of starting her job in the spring and being overwhelmed with requests from inmates for her to write Mother's Day cards for them. When Father's Day approached a month later, she prepared with a big box of cards. To her surprise, not one prisoner approached her for a card since, as she realized, they had no fathers.[25]

The father wound can be deep. Sometimes it heals to know God as father, because you had a good one or because you need a good one; sometimes it only wounds further. I am inclined to think that for Jesus, calling God "Father" was inspired by the unconditional love he knew from the man who adopted him as his own.

While in seminary I went to a workshop led by Walter Wink, a well-known bible scholar and theologian at the time. Wink pointed out that all the verbs in the Lord's Prayer are in the imperative tense. They are not meant to be said in a tentative, pretty please voice. They are commands. Wink asked us to scream the Lord's Prayer. We shouted and demanded the verbs: come, give, forgive, lead, deliver! For some this was very upsetting and they dropped out. In one of his books Wink wrote, "Praying is rattling God's cage and waking God up and setting God free." Wink said prayer is like "giving God water and food and cutting the ropes off his hands and manacles off his feet and washing the caked sweat from his eyes and then watching God swell with life and vitality and energy and following wherever God goes."[26] It is fascinating to approach the Lord's Prayer as fuel for God.

---

25   Thankful to Chaplain Carey Cash for this story.
26   *The Powers That Be: Theology for a New Millennium* by Walter Wink, copyright 1999.

Though I have prayed The Lord's Prayer since I was a child, at sixty I started saying one line of it differently. "Thy will be done." For most of my life I prayed this line with resignation and gritted teeth, with the subtext: "God, help me accept your will, because it sure isn't mine."

I hear people say "Thy will be done" when someone dies, indicating that the death was God's will and not the desire of the one who prays. God's will is seen as tough, perplexing, and a burden to bear.

A professor at Duke Divinity School, Christopher Beeley, lifted that burden for me. He opened a door that sent sunlight and fresh air flooding into the Lord's Prayer. Beeley understands that praying for God's will to be done is not because God's will has prevailed, but because God's will is not being done. Whatever mess or pain we are in is most likely *not* God's will.

Now my subtext is, "God, please, let your will be done because your will is always for wholeness, justice, and peace. We need your will."

Jesus teaches the Lord's Prayer as part of the Sermon on the Mount. He speaks to people who are poor and downtrodden. When he prays "Give us this day our daily bread," the struggle is real. Jesus preaches to people for whom a daily loaf of bread is a symbol of having enough. We rarely are in need of bread, but we still need to be filled. Hope, dignity, respect, kindness, and love are filling and nourishing, and can stop a hunger for having and proving and taking more. Forgiveness can be life-giving food as well. The Lord's Prayer undercuts any notion that the coming of the kingdom will involve the destruction of our enemies. Forgive us as we forgive others. The Lord's Prayer leaves no room for revenge.

"Do not lead us into temptation, but deliver us from evil" is a difficult line to parse. It suggests that God is prone to lead us astray, to try to trip us up. Pope Francis thinks the words should be changed to "Let us not fall into temptation."

The Greek word for *lead* means "to carry inward" or "to bring inside." It is the same word used in the gospel's story of the paralytic whose friends lower him through the roof to bring him to Jesus. He is led to Jesus. This reframes how I pray now: "Don't let temptation under my roof, don't allow temptation to enter my house or heart."

The Lord's Prayer ends with a doxology that Jesus didn't teach: "For yours is the kingdom, and the power, and the glory." It is a radical conclusion because it claims for God three things that the Roman Empire and emperor would love to claim for themselves. It is an upraised fist against every earthly authority that claims to be absolute—along with an upraised hand and heart in praise and commitment to God.

A parishioner told me a story about her granddaughter. The kindergartener said she wanted to be an artist, just like God. The grandparent asked, "What do you mean 'just like God'?" The child explained, "You know. Like it says in the prayer. Our Father, who does art in heaven."

Sometimes we need a five-year-old to clear things up for us.

PERICOPE (2009)

The members of my family like to joke that they are just fodder for sermons and devotions, but they never have actually written anything for me … until this summer. Our daughter, Caroline, returned from Tanzania and handed me four pages. Across the top of the first page she wrote "Devotion ideas for Mom."

Caroline listened to Swahili tapes for months, but it wasn't until she had spent several days in Tanzania that she noticed the word "please" was not only a word she hadn't learned yet, but she hadn't heard the word used yet either.

She heard Tanzanians say "thank you" (*asante*) all the time. Another word she heard repeatedly was "welcome" (*karibu*), even long after her first few days there. "I welcome you to my home." "I welcome you to my food." "I welcome you to sit with me." She realized that the Tanzanians' generosity eliminated the need for the word "please." If someone has already offered you something, there is no reason to make a request for it.

The people Caroline met were always offering their hand and drawing her in. Every day she walked a half-mile to the school where she taught, and every day children who did not know her would run up, take her hand, and walk with her to school.

We pride ourselves in the South for our hospitality, yet we have much to learn from Tanzanians, some who live in homes with bare floors and no running water. God's hospitality and generosity is much like the Tanzanians'. God welcomes us long before we ask; God offers his hand to walk with us each day. We are not required to say "please," but I bet God appreciates "thank you."

CHAPTER 16

JUMPING THE SHARK

OF ALL THE stories in the gospels about Jesus, only one stands out to me as "jumping the shark."

Not the feeding of five thousand or walking on water, or even the resurrection. It is the transfiguration that comes across as contrived and overdone.

"Jumping the shark" is an idiom coined by Hollywood. It describes when a successful television series, losing its mojo and viewers, inserts a preposterous storyline in a frantic attempt to regain prominence and publicity. The phrase originated when the once wildly popular television series *Happy Days*, tanking in the ratings, aired an episode in which the Fonz jumped a shark while waterskiing. I like linking Jesus and Fonzie.

Jesus takes Peter, James, and John to the top of a mountain and the gospellers tell us that Jesus undergoes a transfiguration. They describe his appearance as if they were writing copy for a laundry detergent commercial. Matthew says "His face shone and his clothes became as white as light." (Matthew 17:2) Luke calls them "dazzling white." (Luke 9:29) Mark reports that "his clothes became radiant, intensely white, as no one on earth could bleach them." (Mark 9:3)

In addition to Jesus getting whitewashed, long-dead rock stars Moses and Elijah show up and talk to Jesus. The entire scenario is flashy and farfetched. If it was intended to prove Jesus's divinity and VIP status, it jumped the shark. Did Peter, James, and John really need this display of divine firepower to be convinced that Jesus was the Anointed, the Messiah?

Peter, James, and John bumble and stumble in the story of the transfiguration. They quickly realize they are in way over their heads and fall to the ground on their faces. Even after what they have seen Jesus do and say, this event appears to take the cake. Maybe they are like me, and their eyes don't know whether to roll or pop out of their heads.

It's not that Jesus undergoes a change, but *how* that leaves me cold.

Jesus's physical matter is modified. The disciples fall to the ground not because Jesus shines in a euphemistic way. As a colleague put it, "some weird shit was going on."

I watched a documentary entitled *My Octopus Teacher*. It won an Oscar in 2021. A man who can hold his breath underwater for over six minutes befriends an octopus and takes us to a world on earth that is bizarre and vast and magical. It's not a cartoon. Its reality called me up short. Who am I to question what is possible?

A phenomenon called *microchimerism* describes a metaphysical transfiguration that likely has occurred within me and millions of others. Microchimerism is the presence of DNA that can be found in our bones and organs that comes from people other than our parents.

Microchimerism commonly occurs after someone receives a blood transfusion or transplant. It also occurs between a mother and the baby she carries. Small numbers of cells traffic across the placenta during pregnancy, from the baby to the mother, and from the mother to the baby.

Science tells us that the baby's cells can persist in a woman's body well into her old age, and this is true even if the baby she carried didn't live to be born. The cells of that child stay with her, resonating in ways that mothers have known intuitively throughout time.[27]

---

27   "Baby's cells Can Manipulate Mom's Body for Decades" by Viviane Callier, *Smithsonian, September 2, 2015*

The makeup of every person who has miscarried or lost a child can be changed irrevocably by the experience, but how fascinating it is to realize the loss is also lived—or remembered and stored—by altering the *physical* makeup of the mother as well.

And that's not all.

Not only can the baby's cells exist in a mother's blood, bone marrow, skin, kidney, and liver, the cells appear to treat the mother when she is sick or injured. A liver biopsy in one woman revealed thousands of male cells determined to be from a baby boy she had miscarried twenty years earlier, and these cells helped her recover. There's evidence that fetal cells can provide some protection from certain cancers. Fetal cells can contribute stem cells. They can generate new neurons in the mother's brain and even help to heal heart disease.[28]

Most of us are not transfigured in the blink of an eye as Jesus was. Our lives are changed and shaped and transformed slowly by our experiences and choices—the good ones and the bad ones, the humiliating one and the exhilarating ones, the joyous ones and the sad ones. Our transfiguration takes place more like the lapping of waves on the beach that gradually changes the shoreline completely. You might not notice the influence unless you stick around for a while. Say, a lifetime.

We who partake in the bread and wine of communion hope to experience a change within us.

Perhaps microchimerism is a scientific word to describe our mystical exchange at the Eucharist. We eat the bread and wine, the body and blood of Christ, praying that Christ "may dwell in us and we in Him." (Book of Common Prayer, page 336)

---

28   "Scientists Discover Children's Cells Living in Mothers' Brains" by Robert Martone, *Scientific American,* December 4, 2012

The Last Supper was a celebration of Passover, a remembrance of God's intervention and saving help for their Jewish ancestors. The story of the liberation from slavery in Egypt resides deep in their bones. The Eucharist points not only to the past but to the future, providing a holy meal that bears the potential to heal, forgive, strengthen, and transfigure us on every level down to our marrow. Such a hope and expectation could be interpreted as jumping the shark. It is certainly an improbable leap of faith.

Maybe the story of the transfiguration was not meant to be told. Maybe it was intended as a private summit of the Holy Trinity. Matthew, Mark, and Luke place the transfiguration as Jesus leaves the safety of Galilee and sets his face for the terrors of Jerusalem. Perhaps the person who needed convincing was Jesus. Maybe this was a divine pep talk, a reminder to Jesus that he is not alone, that he is backed by a star-studded cast who went toe to toe with the despots of their day but who also required God's reassurance and encouragement along the way.

Could all that dazzling brightness on the mountaintop have been so that the Light of the World could see it for himself?

For a sliver of time, what had been shuttered shone bright, and a ribbon of glory leapt across the crest of a Galilean hilltop.

Pericope (2020)

The Lone Ranger was misnamed. He wasn't alone at all. He didn't defeat the bad guys or escape from danger on his own. He had the help of his friend Tonto as well as his horse, Silver.

As God said in Genesis 2, "It is not good to be alone."

In fact, it is not healthy either. On the Italian island of Sardinia, people live very long lives. Sardinia's ratio of centenarians in the population is ten times that of the United States.

A study done on the genetics and lifestyle of the Sardinians revealed that genetics contributed to only 25% of their longevity. The lifestyle factors that contributed to their long lives? Here are the top five:

1. Social integration
2. Close relationships
3. Stop smoking
4. Stop boozing
5. Flu vaccine[29]

Who would have thought exercise would rank behind the flu vaccine? Even more surprising, who would have thought that social integration would be the most influential factor?

Close relationships are the people in your life who call the doctor when you are sick and sit with you until you get well. Social integration refers to the people you interact with as you move through your day. Do you talk with your mail carrier, the cashier, the neighbor who walks by your house, the security guard at your office?

---

29   "The Secret to Living Longer May Be Your Social Life," TED talk by Susan Pinker, 2017.

Bill Baynard was confined to his home for years. When he died, his mail carrier cried upon getting the news. My mail carrier is not going to shed a tear at my demise. When I joined another parishioner, Sally Cooper, in a hospital waiting room, she had learned the names of the strangers sitting near her and bought them lunch.

The people in Sardinia remind us of how we are wired, how we are divinely created to be in relationship, to be connected, to thrive through our interdependence. Saint Paul wrote, "we, who are many, are one body in Christ, and individually we are members of one another." (Romans 12:5)

Who was that masked man? Anything but alone.

CHAPTER 17

HOLY WEEK: PALM SUNDAY

I HAVE A reoccurring nightmare. In the dream, my children and I are in some sort of danger, but instead of shielding or helping my children, I run. I save my own neck first and abandon my children in their greatest hour of need. Ultimately I am seen for who I truly am: a coward, weak, selfish, and the worst mother in the world.

The Palm Sunday liturgy is the church's reoccurring nightmare. It is called the Passion of Christ, with *passion* meaning "suffering." In the reading of the Passion gospel narratives, we too are revealed to be weak and selfish people who, when it comes right down to it, are worried most about saving our own skin above all else and at any cost. In the Palm Sunday nightmare, the innocent is doomed as well, with no one coming to Jesus's aid. According to Matthew, Mark, and Luke, every one of the twelve disciples abandon or betray Jesus. Even the women who follow him to the cross stand at a distance.

The crowd is the constant in Jesus's life. Crowds of people fill the streets of Bethlehem as well as its inns, leaving no room for the holy family to stay. When Jesus is twelve and visiting Jerusalem with his parents for the Passover, he is separated from his parents in the crowd gathered there. A crowd teems the banks of the River Jordan at Jesus's baptism. A crowd is there when the paralytic is lowered through the roof to be healed, when Zacchaeus climbs a tree to see Jesus, and when five thousand sit hungry on a hillside. The crowd on Palm Sunday gathers in joy and glad expectation. As Jesus enters the city, the press of people must have been astounding on the narrow streets of Jerusalem.

The throng waves palm fronds to claim their unabashed allegiance to Jesus and lines the dusty road with their coats. They cry out "Hosanna!" which translates as "save me!" (Matthew 21:8-9)

When my children were infants, they didn't cry out "Hosanna!" from their cribs, but their wails meant the same. Help! Save me! If they did not cry out, they would not have been fed or changed as often as they needed to be. They would not have been held or cuddled as often as they insisted upon. Their ability to cry Hosanna was their lifeline.

It might appear that a hero is needed in our nightmares to save us, to accomplish what we cannot or will not do.

The passion of Jesus on the cross is not to show us Jesus's brave heart, or his extraordinary ability to withstand intense pain, to take a licking and keep on ticking. The greater the suffering does not mean the greater the Savior. There are many others in history who have endured painful, grisly executions. We have only to look at the front page of the newspaper each week. There are people whose pain is not physical per se, but of the heart and mind, and who suffer more than Jesus. One could argue that Jesus's mother, Mary, had the harder path to walk than did her son. Bearing helpless witness to the torture and execution of one's own child might be worse than experiencing the torture, even death, oneself.

By morning after his arrest, the crowd reappears and is disappointed, disenchanted, to see the one they had placed all their hopes upon, stand before them condemned, ridiculed, stripped, powerless. Is this the royalty they honored just days before? The crowd—the only participant in the gospels who accompanies Jesus throughout the length of his days on earth—turns from being an adoring host to a threatening mob. They embody their worst nightmares.

Jesus is not great because he suffered the most, or because of his capacity to endure much suffering. Jesus on the cross is weak, vulnerable, mocked, naked, betrayed, broken, beaten. The passion is not Jesus at his strongest but Jesus at his weakest. And yet therein lies his strength.

Christ chooses to identify with our weaknesses, our pain, our suffering. Jesus suffers and dies alongside sinners, abandoned and alone, a commoner's death, just one of the crowd. He is anyone; he is everyone.

The point of the passion is not for us to so much feel Christ's pain, as it is for us to know that Christ is present with us in our pain, in our brokenness and weakness. Christ hears our cries of Hosanna. We do not suffer alone, and our suffering is transformed by one who suffered like us, not because he was brave or strong enough to endure but as Paul writes in Philippians 2, because Christ emptied himself, humbled himself to take on the nightmare of our own likeness. And when that nightmare ends on the cross, its power to ruin us ends as well. Jesus becomes one with the crowd in all its weakness and failings, and we, those feckless, fickle members of the crowd, ultimately, by God's grace and love, also become one with Christ in his resurrection—the remarkable transformation of suffering, even death, into triumph, into hope, into life anew and unending.

PERICOPE (2019)

At the Highland Games at Grandfather Mountain, I was fascinated by the caber toss. Burly men pick up a telephone pole and launch it in the air, end over end. The winner is not determined by how far the caber is tossed, but by how straight it lands.

This game was derived from when warriors crossed freezing streams in the Scottish Highlands by tossing cabers or tree trunks from one side of the stream to the other to create a bridge. A straight toss was critical because the slightest angle would send the caber into the water to float away.

How we judge anyone or thing to be successful or the winner is significant. We like numbers and measurable results to evaluate our efforts. It is reasonable and fair to want to be effective at what we do. But sometimes it is better to ask "Am I being faithful?" instead of "Am I being effective?"

Should I visit my mother who has dementia if my visits don't seem to improve her situation?

Is singing in the choir wasted time if no one at church reports growing closer to God?

Is the value of tucking my child in bed determined only by how fast she falls asleep?

Can I quantify how much my husband loves me by how frequently he does my bidding?

Our lives are made up of tasks, gestures, activities, and relationships that are not only countless but often count more when they reflect our faithfulness.

My mother is no "better" for my visits, but perhaps I am, and her caregivers too, for receiving my gratitude.

Volunteering might not offer instant gratification, but sharing our gifts and time might be a spiritual practice that cultivates hope and humility.

Spending time tucking a child in bed could delay falling asleep, but maybe a hand cupping a face and tender whispers of affection at the close of the day provide warmth and connection that carry into adulthood.

Keeping track of how often our spouse follows our instructions could be a sign of their love, but all the unbidden kindnesses and thoughtfulness can reveal a deeper commitment to us.

Being effective is a very good goal. Being faithful is just good.

Chapter 18

Holy Week: Jesus Overturns the Tables

In the fall of 2017 my husband and I sat down to watch *Saturday Night Live*. We don't stay up late enough to watch it live so we record it to enjoy at a more palatable hour: right after 7:00 p.m. *Jeopardy*. One of the SNL skits was a commercial advertising Woke Jeans. When the skit was over, Tim and I looked at each other quizzically. The next day there was a photo in the newspaper of Carolina Panther football player Shaq Thompson's shoes, which had the words "Stay Woke" written on them. I googled "woke" to see what I was missing.

If doesn't take much to be more hip than I am. I was delighted with the definition of my new vocabulary word. Woke: to be aware of other's people's experiences, perspectives, and struggles, particularly around issues of social justice. The word first became popular as part of the Black Lives Matter movement and referred to its efforts to awaken us all to vast and persistent racial inequities embedded in American systems that oppress people of color and tacitly advantage white people. The term *woke* is appropriated to any number of ways that people are opening their eyes to things that are Just. Not. Right. For instance, thousands of victims of sexual harassment are making us all woke to a culture that tolerates unchecked abuses of power and routinely victimizes victims. The increasing number of mass shootings is making us woke to the accessibility of weapons that are expressly designed to create carnage and were used by over half the killers in mass shootings.

The term *woke* is new to me but not the concept. I have had many experiences of becoming woke, and so have you. We become woke when we experience pain or hardship, or when those we love do. When someone near and dear to us dies, we often become woke to how important it is to reach out to those who are grieving, to show up, to attend funerals, to call and say I am thinking of you because those things helped us. Whether it is an experience with addiction, mental illness, physical disability, dementia, bullying, job loss, infertility, divorce, or just being new to town, our challenges awaken us as to how we can help others who suffer as we have. But it is harder to be woke to circumstances and suffering we have never experienced ourselves.

That was Amos the prophet's challenge. He preaches to those who were oblivious to, and often complicit in, the suffering of others around them. His audience is sound asleep to the egregious inequalities of their culture and their spirituality. Amos proclaims to the wealthy and pious: "Let justice roll down like waters, and righteousness like an everflowing stream." (Amos 5:24)

In the Garden of Gethsemane, Jesus asks only one thing of his disciples at the end: stay awake with me. (Matthew 26:38)

Jesus was woke, and much of his mission was to awaken his followers. Jesus exposes systems and cultural norms that robbed people of their humanity. He opens his ministry saying "The Spirit of the Lord is upon me. He has anointed me to bring good news to the poor. He has sent me to proclaim release to the captives and recovery of sight to the blind, to let the oppressed go free, to proclaim the year of the Lord's favor." (Luke 4:18-19)

Jesus shakes people awake to injustices when he dines with lepers and tells parables that value the lost, the last, and the least. Jesus spoke woke: Love your enemies. Lose your life in order to save it. Whoever wants to be great must first be servant of all. The meek shall inherit the earth. He starts his ministry quietly turning water into wine and closes it with a bang turning over the moneychangers' tables in the temple.

Systemic evil, not individual sin, upsets Jesus the most. With Passover around the corner, he stands in Jerusalem's great temple amid all the bleating lambs waiting to become bleeding sacrifices. Faithful pilgrims scrimped and saved their whole life to travel far and offer a sacrifice at the temple, only to arrive and find that neither their money nor their animal was acceptable. They are asked to buy a temple-approved animal for sacrifice with temple currency, and the exchange rate and the price of animals are exorbitant and exploitive. Jesus not only flips the tables, he flips the entire system. Jesus becomes the new temple—the place where God is found, and he also becomes the lamb, the sacrifice to end all sacrifices.

When Jesus is described as making a whip of cords, driving the moneychangers, sheep, and cattle out of the temple, emptying their cash registers and overturning their tables, I am reminded of recent protests against injustices and the smashing of windows. Nothing indicates Jesus took something that wasn't his, but he *is* protesting and he is damaging property. Jesus could see how the social, political, economic, and religious systems of his day were looting the poor of dignity, opportunity, and equity, all in the name of sustaining order and righteousness. Jesus called this pointing out the speck in someone else's eye while disregarding the plank in our own eye.

Jesus woke listeners to social injustices. He also woke them to the unimaginable and unmerited grace of God.

I heard The Reverend David Zahl describe grace as the surprising presence of love in the very moment that we feel the most judged, the most vulnerable and lost. At the temple, authorities set up tables to rob the faithful and take advantage of them. But grace is just the opposite. Grace is the moment tables are turned *for* us, love given when we least deserve it, welcome and acceptance offered at the brink of being outcast and rejected, peace provided in the midst of battle.

A nine-year-old boy moved to a new town just before the start of school. He was anxious, and mad about having to leave his friends, and he couldn't imagine being happy again. On the first day of class, his mother drove him to school. He was overwhelmed by all the new faces and names to remember. He pined for his friends at his old school where everything was familiar.

On the second day, he had to ride the school bus. He was terrified. He could hear the chatter and laughter of children as the bus pulled up to his stop. It made him feel worse. He climbed onto the bus and looked for an empty seat. Most seats were full, and some children had placed their backpack in open seats beside them. No one seemed to notice or look at him. Then the boy heard someone call his name. A hand waved near the back of the bus.

He walked down the aisle toward the boy who had his arm raised, but as he got closer, the boy's arm came down. Panic filled the new boy's heart. Was the boy waving at someone else? Was this some sort of mean trick?

Then he realized that the boy who waved had pulled his hand down in order to pat the seat next to him. "I saved a seat for you," he said with smile. Fifty years later, that new boy in town is a man who says, "I still remember something being born in me in that moment. That was my first experience of salvation. For me, salvation means Jesus is saving a seat for me on the bus."[30]

Jesus spoke truth and woke minds and broke through hearts. I like the image of Jesus in the temple, forceful, fired up, and flipping things upside down so I might be saved by the foolish wisdom and grace of God. But I also know Jesus can turn toward me, see my fears, and pat the seat next to him. The Oxford English Dictionary added the word "woke" to its pages, defining it as being alert to injustice. Another addition to the dictionary at the same time was the phrase "come to Jesus," defined as a meeting or discussion intended to create a significant shift in the current way of thinking or doing something. Being woke nearly always involves a come-to-Jesus moment. Jesus still asks those who follow him: stay awake with me.

---

30   I was unable to find or remember the source of this story.

Pericope (2017)

I participated in the Women's March last Saturday. There were lots of clever signs, but my favorite was the one that pointed out that the word "love" is spelled backward in the middle of the word "rEVOLution."

The bible's definition of love usually involves going against the grain, the flow, the tide. We are often asked to do what makes no sense. To be first by taking last place. To believe that *anyone* can be redeemed. To be generous givers instead of anxious hoarders. To hope in possibilities unseen.

The former Archbishop of Canterbury, Rowan Williams, tells the story of when he served an interim stint at a parish. Williams writes:

> Just before the new vicar arrived, the bishop rang me up to say, "You will have to call a special PCC [Parish Church Council] meeting because the man who is coming as the new vicar has just left his wife, and you had better explain that to them." So I did, and waited, bracing myself for the worst. The first comment that came was from a very sober-sided churchwarden, an ex-military man, one of the more conservative, middle-class members of the congregation, who shook his head and said, "I think this man is going to need all the help we can give him." I felt deeply converted by that response—surprised and moved and in touch with the giving God, with a giftedness in the man whose first response, to what was really quite a disorienting bit of news, was generosity.[31]

The kind of generous heart that Jesus lived is what we are called to as his disciples. When we walk love backward in the world, it moves us all forward.

---

31   I was unable to find my source of this story.

CHAPTER 19

HOLY WEEK: THE ANOINTING IN BETHANY

"YOU IS SMART. You is kind. You is important." Those are the words in the opening scene of the movie *The Help*. Aibileen, who works as a maid, repeats those words over and over again to the two-year-old under her care. She intended for her words to coat and protect the child from the neglect and disdain of the child's own mother. I see Aibileen's words as a form of anointing, much like the physical anointing that Jesus received in the days before his death.

Mary, of Mary and Martha fame, anoints Jesus with costly perfume just days before Jesus enters Jerusalem, is arrested, and is killed. She is accused of being wasteful, and Jesus defends her actions. This story is one of my all-time favorites. A version of this story is told in all four gospels. (Matthew 26:6-13, Mark 14:3-9, Luke 7:36-50, John 12:1-8)

In Matthew and Mark's gospels, Jesus even proclaims that she has done a beautiful thing for him.

I cannot think of another story in the gospels when someone ministers to Jesus; Jesus is usually the one doing the ministering. But here, the woman's extravagant gesture seems to encourage, even comfort Jesus. And with Jerusalem looming ahead, her actions come at just the right time. That Jesus is about to do something difficult is an understatement.

To anoint someone is to daub, smear, or pour oil, perfume, or water on someone's head, face, or even feet as a sign of welcome, hospitality, or honor. In biblical times, kings were literally anointed, with oil poured over their heads, to signify their selection as ruler. *Messiah* translates as "the anointed one" in Hebrew, and *Christ* means the same in Greek.

To call Jesus the Messiah or Christ is to say he is the one anointed by God, the chosen one, the one set aside to lead his people into peace and glory.

Perhaps Mary sees Jesus for who he truly is and what that is going to cost him in the days ahead. Mary is criticized for wasting something valuable, but she is actually the only one who understands that the cost of the perfume is nothing next to what the future will cost for Jesus.

In some parts of the world, anointing is still a hospitality custom. Anointing is part of our baptisms and healing service, but otherwise we don't practice physical anointing much anymore. Yet we are still called to anoint one another in much the same way that Mary anointed Jesus and Aibileen anointed her charge. For I think that preparing and empowering one another to do something difficult, reminding one another that we are chosen and beloved, especially in the face of challenge, is still very much a part of how we minister to one another. We might not pour perfume over each other's heads or feet, but when we decant words of praise, hope, encouragement, and love, we anoint one another. When we endow each other with courage and faith, we anoint one another. When we prepare and commission each other to be our best selves, we anoint one another.

I think of the parent outside the classroom on the first day of kindergarten, anointing his or her anxious child with encouraging words that all will be well, with a reassuring hand on each shoulder and a look that conveys love and confidence. Imagine the powerful and costly anointings that must take place in military airport hangars as families bid their soldiers goodbye. Worship is meant to anoint and equip us for whatever challenges lay outside the church doors.

Once when our son at fourteen did something stupid and unkind, I forced him to make a face-to-face apology to those he offended, who included two adults. Rob visibly shrank at the idea. But Mom, he said, that man's garage is full of guns! Rob was nervous, fearful, embarrassed—and mad at his parents. But I knew the people he would apologize to, and I knew they would be kind. None of our lecturing (though we still lectured) and none of the punishments we could impose (though we still imposed them) would do more for the boy's soul and growth into becoming a man than to ask for and experience forgiveness from those he had wronged.

I drove him to the family's neighborhood. He asked me to stop a few blocks away. He walked the rest of the way as if to his execution. When he returned from making amends, he collapsed in the car and blurted, "My pits are soaked I was sweating so bad." I was proud of him, and a little proud of myself for making him do it. Saying he was sorry and receiving their forgiveness was an anointing. It restored his dignity and revealed to him the incomparable value of mercy.

When Mary anoints Jesus, she doesn't consider that a little dab would do. She uses a pound of perfume made from a precious flower found at the base of the Himalayas. Judas says the perfume should have been sold and the money given to the poor. But Jesus says, "Leave her alone. You always have the poor with you but you do not always have me." (Matthew 26:11) Jesus knows there will always be petitions for our time and money. There will always be valid and compelling reasons to be prudent and cautious. The novelist Reynolds Price was asked several years ago in a radio interview what regrets he had in his life. He said his only regrets were his "economies"—those times when he was small, when he held back, when he was less generous and more guarded.

Who has time to write a letter, read to a child, listen to a friend, plant flowers, say I am sorry? When my children were small and seemingly bottomless pits of need, I could translate Jesus's words to say, "You will always have the laundry with you, but you will not always have these children happy, eager, and open to receive the anointing of your love and attention." Unrelenting bids for our time and energy can draw us away from the people and things that really matter.

A few days after Mary pours perfume on Jesus's feet, Jesus gathers with his twelve disciples and washes their feet. Perhaps the experience of

Mary washing his feet inspires him to do the same for the twelve. The experience is so powerful for Jesus, he wants others to share it. When someone steps up and spends costly words, time, effort, or love to say that your health, your wholeness, your dignity, your capacity to hope and trust is important to me, *then* we grow, *then* we bloom like a rare Himalayan flower. And when we do the same for others, then once more, like Mary, we minister to Jesus.

PERICOPE (2018)

Spiritual practices are about "surviving your twenties or forties or eighties and not becoming a jerk in the process," writes Brian McLaren in his book *Finding Our Way Again.*[32]

I like McLaren's bluntness. A lot happens to us. It's easy to become bitter, jaded, negative, angry, and unpleasant to be around. McLaren says that spiritual practices give birth to a person we are proud of becoming, a best friend, a hero, a loving beloved, and beloved lover. When our character is left untended, he says we will become "a stale room, an obnoxious child, a vacant lot filled with thorns and weeds."[33]

I met Lillian thirty years ago. She lived at a nursing home. Multiple sclerosis had paralyzed her from the neck down. She had no family in town. One day I visited her, and a man was there feeding her fried chicken. He told me his mother used to live across the hall but had died years ago. He and Lillian became friends. On Sundays he read the newspaper to her.

Another friend rolled Lillian's wheelchair to a movie theater down the street to see *Amadeus.* Lillian's eyes shone talking about that day. I wondered how a woman confined to her bed, who could not even wave her hand, could make friends with a man across the hall. What sort of dynamism could draw strangers into her room, and then keep them coming back again and again?

Lillian never complained to me. She was cheery and every day she asked the staff to apply lipstick and rouge on her face. I brought her communion but didn't visit nearly often enough. Each time, without

---

32   *Finding Our Way Again: The Return of the Ancient Practices* by Brian McLaren, page 14, copyright 2008.

33   Ibid, pages 11-12.

fail, she would direct me to the top drawer of a chest in her room and ask me to take out her pledge envelope and five dollars—her monthly pledge. I felt odd following her instructions. How could I take money from her? The church would survive without her five dollars each month. But I realized it meant something to her to give it, to offer it, to be a part of something bigger and beyond her four walls, to feel connected instead of alone, and be contributing instead of taking.

Lillian died more than twenty years ago. She never became a jerk, but no one would have blamed her if she had. I don't know what her spiritual practices were, but clearly somewhere along the way, she had tended to the garden of her soul and character.

CHAPTER 20

HOLY WEEK: MAUNDY THURSDAY

"THE LAST NIGHT."

It's a dramatic moniker. And the last night of Jesus's life is that and more. It is a night of whispers, farewells, tears, mystery, shadows, and secrets.

Even before the sun comes up, clandestine events take place on Maundy Thursday. It is time for Passover, and Jewish law required every man living within a ten-mile radius of Jerusalem to celebrate Passover in the city. But Jerusalem has become dangerous for Jesus, especially at night. His enemies are vocal and powerful and antsy to arrest him. Jesus needs to enter the city unnoticed, but the problem is, to reverse John Lennon's quote, Jesus is more popular than the Beatles. Jesus needs a private place to celebrate Passover where the authorities cannot find him. The homes of his family and close friends are surely under surveillance.

Jesus instructs Peter and John to go to Jerusalem ahead of him. "Behold, when you have entered the city, meet a man carrying a jar of water. Follow him into the house which he enters." (Mark 14:2-3) Very cloak and dagger. Jesus had planned ahead. The man with the watering jar on his head? Obviously not someone Peter or John would recognize. The jar was the red carnation in the lapel, a way to distinguish the man. Getting water from the well was a woman's job, not a man's. He would stand out in a crowd. Without any words between them, the man with the jar leads Peter and John to a house, but not his own.

Jesus tells Peter and John to follow the man into the house and "Tell the householder, 'The Teacher says to you, Where is the guest room where I am to eat the Passover with my disciples?' And he will show you a large upper room furnished; there make ready.'" (Mark 14:14-15) Notice that Jesus's name is not mentioned. He is referred to in code as the "Teacher." Jesus describes the room they will find, and either he has seen the room before or had it described to him or was very specific about what sort of room he wanted. Jesus goes to great lengths to eat the Passover in Jerusalem unobserved. He is aware how dangerous it is for him to be there. Jesus isn't trying to get arrested. He isn't resigned to this being his last night. If it were not for the betrayal of Judas, he might have pulled it off.

But the night holds many secrets, and Judas knows one of them, and sometime, somewhere, Jesus knows it too. Betrayal is imminent. This is indeed the last night.

Jesus girds himself with a towel, takes a basin of water, and washes his disciples' feet. Scripture records Peter's embarrassment and astonishment at the very idea. "You shall never wash my feet," Peter recoils. (John 13:8)

Yet it is not Peter's reaction but Judas's that intrigues me. The bible is silent on it. It is eerie to think about what was going through the mind of both Judas and Jesus, as one cradled the foot of the other in the basin, both knowing a terrible secret. When Jesus later forgives those who nail him to the cross, he was practiced. He had already washed the feet of the one whose betrayal was deepest.

In doing so, Jesus demonstrates servant leadership. Wikipedia credits a Mr. Greenleaf from Terre Haute, Indiana, as the founder of the servant leadership movement, but I'm pretty sure it was a Mr. BarJoseph from Nazareth.

Jesus does more than tell his disciples how to lead—he shows them. He dons the garb and picks up the tools of a servant. He reveals a leadership model where the leader says to followers, "I work for you." In this model, workers feel appreciated and heard. The leader casts a compelling vision that includes developing each worker's potential and empowering them to do their best work. This theology of leadership is as difficult as it is rewarding.

Jesus promises to help. He tells his disciples at table their last night together, "In this world you will have trouble. But take heart! I have overcome the world." (John 16:33) After bewildering them by washing their feet, he blows their minds when he lifts the bread and wine and says, "This is my body. This is my blood." (Mark 14:22-24)

Altogether a very busy night.

When we eat steak and potatoes, the food enters our body and becomes part of us. When we eat the bread and wine of communion, Jesus promises that he becomes part of us. Surely the disciples were stunned by Jesus inviting them to drink blood because that was verboten for Jews. Many of the kosher laws were requirements to remove blood from the diet.

Dr. Paul Brand was a missionary doctor in India in the 1950s. His young family accompanied him. An epidemic of measles struck the Indian village where he lived, and one of Dr. Brand's daughters came down with the disease. Word quickly went out in the village that Dr. Brand's other daughter, an infant, was at great risk of becoming infected, and needed the "blood of an overcomer." His baby girl needed serum from someone who had contracted measles and recovered. The blood of an overcomer. Such a person was found, serum was made, and Dr. Brand's daughter lived. She overcame measles not by her own strength and resistance, but by a battle that had taken place within someone else.[34]

That's how immunizations work. Our bodies receive the proper artillery needed to battle diseases and quickly overwhelm them before they can even be detected. Flannery O'Connor titled her first novel *Wise Blood*, and that is indeed what immunizations make our blood—wise, prepared, equipped to fight off and protect us from disease.

---

34   *In His Image* by Paul Brand and Philip Yancey, pages 94-95, copyright 1984.

Jesus offers us his wise blood in the eucharistic wine—blood that has not only overcome the world, but death and suffering, and every temptation and fear that diminishes and burdens us. We receive the victory of a battle we did not fight.

I don't like sodas or seltzers. My favorite drink, believe it or not, is Kool-Aid, or flavored water. When I was in middle school, I went to the Jeff Frank Tennis Camp at Davidson college. This was back before anybody used sun screen, so we burned and blistered on the unshaded court. Also at that time, drinking water was seen as a treat not a necessity. We roasted in the sun and the sweat dripped off as we ran drills. For our mid-morning break, we were finally given something to drink. Guess what it was? Ice cold Kool-Aid. Nothing else tasted so good. Sometimes I think about how that drink made me feel when I sip from the communion cup. Relief. Repair. Recover.

The communion meal intends to shape us into a particular kind of people. As we share the meal each week, we become the sign of God's presence in the world, and that presence is a serving presence. We are fed and strengthened to be sent out into the world to serve, and not to serve in a way that suggests we have all the goods and answers, and aren't we kind to share them with the poor unfortunate? We are washers of feet, for Christ's sake. We are washers of feet, for *Christ's* sake. The disciple Peter does not get it at first. He doesn't want Jesus to wash his feet. But Jesus needed Peter to know the true meaning of discipleship, and Jesus needs me to know it too.

Jesus does not skip to the cross. Before daybreak, Jesus will sweat blood and plead to live another day. But in the end, he trusts God completely, loves his friends completely, and gives himself completely.

Faith means trusting Jesus's way of being in the world. And on his last night, Jesus's way becomes clearer than ever. We begin with a bowl of water and a towel, a bit of bread and a sip of wine.

PERICOPE (2016)

I came down the steps into the Memorial Garden one summer day wearing my vestments. I anticipated meeting a family any moment for the interment of their loved one's ashes in the garden. I did not recognize four people gathered around one of the garden benches. They were dressed casually, in shorts, one man in a tank top. Two women sat on the bench; one leaned over to pull a drink out of a small cooler. The other woman unwrapped a sandwich.

"Hello," I greeted them. "Are you here for the burial?"

They looked at me blankly.

"We are having a graveside service here in a few minutes," I added.

"Oh, I'm sorry. We didn't know," said the woman with the sandwich. She introduced herself and the others, who were her siblings. "Both our parents are buried here by this bench. None of us live in town, but once a year we meet here and bring a picnic to this garden to be with them."

I told them it warmed my heart to learn of their tradition. Truly it did. The Memorial Garden is a place of the living and the dead, and their picnic embodied that beautifully.

What separates the living and the dead often appears vast and impenetrable, yet I experience it to be thin and permeable, particularly by love and courage, by prayer and praise.

That is our Christian hope, and what we celebrate every Sunday at a picnic we call the Eucharist.

CHAPTER 21

HOLY WEEK: BARABBAS

No DOUBT THE family and friends of Barabbas experienced a very different version of Good Friday.

When the sun set on Good Friday, Jesus's family and friends went home with heavy hearts. But somewhere else in the city, a festive homecoming was underway. Barabbas and all who loved him remembered the day as one of unexpected joy, freedom, and new life. They told a story not of mourning, but of celebration, a day when Barabbas escaped certain death, the story of a man who was inexplicably pardoned and released at the eleventh hour.

If Barabbas's mother were in the crowd that day, she would certainly have cried out for her son's release and for Jesus to be crucified instead. Maybe she stood not too far from Jesus's mother in the crowd.

Who was Barabbas? What do we know about him? According to Mark and Luke's gospel, Barabbas is an insurrectionist and murderer. (Mark 15:7, Luke 23:19) John calls him a bandit and Matthew says Barabbas is notorious, suggesting that his crimes are well known. (John 18:40, Matthew 27:16) John's gospel adds that Barabbas took part in a rebellion. When Peter preaches from the temple steps in Acts 3, he calls Barabbas a murderer. The bible does not cut Barabbas any slack. But it is possible Barabbas is misunderstood and that his motives were noble. He might have been a Zealot, a freedom fighter, a revolutionary seeking the overthrow of the oppressive Romans, and in the process killed someone, all in the cause of freedom. Or he may have been just a really, really bad dude.

Barabbas's name is easy to translate, even if you aren't a Hebrew scholar. The Hebrew word *Bar* means son. We are familiar with that word from the term *bar mitzvah*, which means "son of the covenant." We are also familiar with the Hebrew word *Abba*, meaning father. Earlier in Mark, Jesus in the Garden of Gethsemane prays, "*Abba*, Father, if possible take this cup from me," (Mark 14:36) and Paul, on two occasions, refers to God as *Abba*, Father. (Romans 8:15, Galatians 4:6) So Barabbas's name translates as "son of the father." Reminds me of how our family called our cat "Kitty."

When Pilate stands up and asks the crowd whom to save, he is giving them a choice between Jesus, the Son of the Father, using capital letters, or Barabbas, son of the father, lowercase. Jesus of Nazareth is described as God incarnate, the Holy Spirit in the flesh, and Barabbas is the world incarnate, the human spirit in the flesh. Barabbas, by his very name, represents all of the children of the father who are given unmerited pardon and released when Jesus is condemned. Barabbas is a symbol of all of us notorious bandits, rebels, murderers of life and joy, insurrectionists, well-intended seekers of justice, and bad dudes who have tried to save ourselves with disastrous results. Jesus's condemnation not only seals Barabbas's salvation, but ours as well.

When the crowd cries out for Barabbas's release, they are in essence calling out for their own release. Free Barabbas! Or free the children of God! It is the same cry the crowds made on Palm Sunday as Jesus entered Jerusalem. "Hosanna!" they shouted, or "Save me!" Don't most of our prayers say the same thing? God, save me, release me, free me or someone I love?

We can all use some saving and release. Shame, guilt, deep sadness, or disappointment weighs all of us down in some measure, and cripples too many of us. Anxiety, fear, or unfair expectations are effective prison bars, blocking us from considering or seeking or trusting in new possibilities. In Richard Rohr's book *Falling Upward,* he writes that suffering is a great spiritual teacher, and that by falling down we move up. Against every survival instinct we have, we grow spiritually much more by doing something wrong than by doing something right.[35]

My son's kindergarten teacher, Mrs. Currie, was a petite ball of fire. When a student made a mistake, her face would light up and she would coo, "I just LOOOVE mistakes!" She saw mistakes as learning opportunities. She didn't tie shame or fear to mistakes like most adults. She understood the difference between a child *making* a mistake and being made to feel like he or she *is* a mistake. She helped her young charges know that falling down could lead to moving forward.

As Barabbas's version of the story tells us, resurrection is not just for the dead; it is also given to the living. Barabbas goes home a free man. Jesus's death changed everything for him. Jesus's death still changes everything. The very worst happens, and yet it will never be enough ultimately to kill hope, love, or life.

---

35   *Falling Upward* by Richard Rohr, page xxii, copyright 2011.

PERICOPE (2020)

While on vacation in Turkey, our tour guide mentioned that he and his wife were naming their new baby "Genghis." "How nice," I said aloud, but inside I was thinking, "Who names their baby after a ruthless killer?" I learned that Genghis Khan is known to some as the greatest conqueror of all time and the ruler over history's largest contiguous empire. A lot depends upon who your history teacher is.

I am pretty sure that no babies get named Judas anymore, but once it was a popular name. One of Jesus's own brothers was named Judas.

Judas saw Jesus walk on water, calm the storm, feed the five thousand, heal the lame and blind. Jesus called Judas to follow him, taught him to pray, trusted him to be the treasurer of the disciples, and commissioned him to heal the sick on his behalf. Jesus washed Judas's feet and sat beside him at the Last Supper. But for thirty pieces of silver, Judas betrayed Jesus, and he did so with a kiss.

Perhaps he was evil. Perhaps he was an unlucky pawn. Maybe he believed he was helping Jesus's cause and accelerating the rise of Jesus's kingdom. On one occasion Judas saw Jesus walk like a beam of light through an angry, murderous mob ready to throw Jesus over a cliff. Surely Jesus could stand up to anything the chief priests could do. After all, they did not have authority to kill.

But we know how this story did go down, and when Judas heard that Jesus was condemned to death, he threw the silver back at the priests. Matthew's gospel tells us Judas repented, and believing he had no better option, he killed himself. Perhaps Judas's biggest mistake was not selling out Jesus for 30 pieces of silver but assuming that his own sin was too great to be forgiven.

The Scottish poet Robert Buchanan wrote a ballad about Judas in which Judas's soul searches for a place to rest and is rejected at every turn until the soul comes to a house in a snowy wood where a wedding is going on. It is the bridegroom who comes to the door, and says to Judas:

> The Holy Supper is spread within,
> And the many candles shine,
> And I have waited long for thee
> Before I poured the wine!
>
> The supper wine is poured at last
> The lights burn bright and fair,
> Iscariot washes the Bridegroom's feet
> And dries them with his hair.[36]

---

36   "The Ballad of Judas Iscariot" by Robert Buchanan first appeared in the February, 1872 issue of *The Saint Paul's Magazine*.

CHAPTER 22

HOLY WEEK: GOOD FRIDAY

ON GOOD FRIDAY in 2005, I was working at Trinity Episcopal School in Charlotte as a chaplain and teacher of faith studies. I planned a Stations of the Cross experience for my fourth and fifth-graders. I pulled into the school parking lot and struggled to wrangle a heavy six-foot wooden cross out of the back of my minivan. The cross was constructed by my colleague the Reverend Fred Paschall. It was an awkward fit into my car, with the bottom of the cross grazing the hatch window and the head of the cross nearly reaching the front seats. Later that day I picked up my daughter and some of her high school friends. As they squeezed around the six-foot cross, it amused me that none of them thought it odd enough to ask why I was driving around with a cross in my minivan.

Outside Trinity School is a wide block-long green median. There are benches on the median, and a man and his wife were sitting on one when he noticed me struggling to get the cross out of my car. He came over to help and graciously carried the cross over to the median for me. I told him I was expecting the fourth-graders to join me outside in a few minutes, and we were going to carry the cross around the entire median block in a service called the Stations of the Cross. He was very interested in what that would look like.

I inquired after the man and his wife. They introduced themselves and told me they were on a journey of their own, albeit a difficult one. Lee, the husband, said they had no place to stay or work.

The Trinity fourth-graders came outside, a chattering, happy group. I handed out copies of the service for the Stations of the Cross. I introduced Lee. They never knew or thought to think that he was a homeless man. Lee helped the children carry the cross at each station and followed along with the service with his copy of the program, his baritone voice blending with the children's voices. Due to the size and weight of the cross, Lee tended to do most of the carrying, with the children assisting. He became the Christ figure in our service, and the children a host of Simons of Cyrene by his side. When the fourth grade finished, they returned to class and the fifth-graders came out. Lee asked if he could do the stations with us again, and I was glad for his help. As we walked the stations, we prayed:

Help us to encourage one another with words and deeds of love and service.

Help us to see the face of our brother and sister in all whom we meet.

Help us to widen the circle of love and compassion in your kingdom on earth.

Help us to reach across all that divides us that we can lift one another up and share the weight of each other's burdens.

Lee reverently bore the cross in a sea of children. I wondered whether we were giving him encouragement. Did we see in his face a brother? Were we widening the circle of love and compassion in God's kingdom? I did know that he encouraged me. I knew *his* circle included me. I knew he had reached out to me and helped me. When the last fifth-grader had left, Lee put the cross back into my car. He didn't ask me for anything, but thanked me and went on his way.

Jesus tells his disciples to take up his cross and follow him. He says whoever loses his life will save it. What will it profit us if we gain the whole world but forfeit our life? To save, you must lose. To gain, you must give up. It is no wonder that the expression, taking up one's cross, has the connotation of burden and loss. When we speak of someone having a cross to bear, we often say it with pity.

A Methodist bishop, Bruce Blake, tells the story of going to the funeral of a Native American held by the Ponca people in Oklahoma. He said, "Prior to the funeral, we went to the Ponca Tribal Center for a time of sharing with the deceased's family. The sharing was not in the form of words, but in the form of giving. If someone needed food, the grieving family gave them a basket of food. Others needed household supplies. The family gave them a basket of supplies. Some had resources to meet their basic needs, so the family gave them blankets and shawls." Blake sat in awe at this expression of giving by a family experiencing grief. He was accustomed, as we are, to just the reverse—friends giving to a bereaved family. When he asked for an explanation of this tradition, he was told, "We believe you can accept death better by giving than by getting. We believe to give until it heals."[37]

Perhaps this comes closer to understanding what Jesus meant by asking his disciples to deny themselves, take up their cross, and follow him. The cross isn't just about how Jesus died; it does not signify only his suffering. The cross is also about how Jesus lived. His life was devoted to others, to caring, respecting, and serving every person as neighbor, to giving as a means to healing. His life was marked by love, peace of mind, prayer, deepening relationships, and service—all in the midst of controversy. To take up Jesus's cross is to take up his way of life. The way of the cross involves forgiving those who hurt you, loving your neighbor as yourself, helping to carry the burdens of others, and giving yourself away for the sake of love.

I think that Lee might not have had much to give to someone else that the world would count as valuable. He literally took up the cross of Christ and carried it for us, and I hope that what he gave me and the children that day—his help, his example, his leadership—brought him some healing and peace—for that is why Jesus asks us to take up his cross. Not to make our life more difficult, but just the opposite. In giving of ourselves, we will find the healing and peace that we so desperately yearn for.

---

37   From an address given by Bishop Bruce Blake to the 2004 General Conference of the United Methodist Church in Pittsburgh, PA.

Pericope (2012)

My daughter teaches second grade in a small town outside of Phoenix, Arizona. By this time of year, Caroline has spun a loving, supportive cocoon of a classroom for her students. They know the rules and expectations and have learned to be considerate, cooperative, and kind to one another. Enter a new boy named Dakota in late January.

Dakota has been in several schools in his short life. He doesn't see the point in following instructions and likes to do things that shock and disrupt his classmates. Dakota is slow to catch on to how things are done in Miss Saunders's classroom. Progress creeps, but this week Dakota raised his hand (instead of blurting out) and answered a question correctly and appropriately (instead of incorrectly and crudely). Before his teacher could commend him, the boy seated beside Dakota patted him on the back and said, "Way to go, Dakota!" In many ways, it is Dakota's classmates as much as his teacher who are helping him to trust that he is in a safe place where people care about him.

Jesus was drawn to the Dakotas of this world, and some would argue he was one himself: stirring up the pot, trespassing boundaries, inserting disorder where there used to be order.

Who or what is the "Dakota" in your life these days? Is it a challenging little boy, a disturbing diagnosis, a painful loss, or a worrisome addition? Generally, the practice of being kind more than being clever, of being patient more than being productive, will give room for others to help us and for God's grace and glory to emerge. Perhaps your Dakota will become President of the United States, or your finest moment, or yet another reminder that you are not alone.

Chapter 23

Holy Week: The Seven Words on the Cross

When I was a teenager, school wasn't closed on Good Friday. My mom would excuse me from class and take me to the Good Friday service at St. Paul's in Winston-Salem. It was a three-hour service and included meditations on the seven words that Jesus spoke on the cross. The seven words are technically seven sentences—or to be even more technical, eight, if you count punctuation.

Two gospels highlight Jesus's divinity at the cross. They depict Jesus in control, kind, and compassionate. The other two gospels hone in on Jesus's stark humanity, his lack of control, his despair and humiliation.

The first of the seven words is in Luke's gospel: *Forgive them for they know not what they do.* (Luke 23:34) Jesus says these words about the soldiers who are nailing him to the cross. These words set the stage for the crucifixion. The violence perpetrated on Jesus will not result in more violence. Forgiveness is the overarching message from Luke's version of the passion. Our natural response to pain is to lash out in return—as the saying goes, hurt people hurt people. Jesus, however, as he often does, shows us a different but highly difficult and divine way.

In the second word, also from Luke, Jesus says to the thief hanging beside him: *Today I will see you in paradise.* (Luke 23:43) It is these words that make me hang my hat on the belief that eternal life begins immediately after death. Saint Paul talks about the dead being asleep for a time until the triumphant last day, but I prefer to put my money on what Jesus said. Again, divine forgiveness coats Luke's passion story as Jesus promises the self-proclaimed guilty bandit a new life that same day.

The third word is taken from John's gospel. This scene is particularly poignant to me as it tells us that Jesus's mother watches her son die. Mary was warned at his birth by the prophet Simeon that her baby would one day pierce her heart, and witnessing his suffering and death was likely worse than the swift work of a sword.

Standing with his mother is the disciple John. "*Woman, here is your son,*" Jesus says to Mary. Then he says to John, "*Here is your mother.*" (John 19:26) In these few words Jesus establishes a whole new understanding of family and connection and responsibility and caring. He does not leave John or his mother bereft or alone, but under one another's wing, with a divine purpose and mission. The beloved community of believers starts here.

The fourth word is the shortest. Jesus says, "*I thirst.*" (John 19:27) We begin to see a little more of Jesus's humanity revealed. He is not a superhuman hanging on the cross, impervious to pain or suffering. This word on the cross is found only in John's gospel. John is also the only gospeller who tells the story of the woman at the well when Jesus declares that he is the source of living water that never fails. And yet at the cross the source of living water is dry and thirsty. In this two-word sentence, John tells us Jesus has poured himself out entirely at the cross. He is spent and has given everything.

The fifth word is likely the most famous. It is recorded in Jesus's own language, perhaps because in the retelling of this story these words stood out above all: *Eli, eli, lema sabachtani! My God, my God, why have you forsaken me?* (Matthew 27:46, Mark 15:34) Here we witness the fulness of Jesus's humanity. He, like so many of us, feels more than just forgotten by God but betrayed. Jesus feels that God has turned his back on him. Some theologians say that God *had* to turn his back on Jesus because he was covered in our sins. But I don't believe it is in God to turn aside from any of us, especially when we suffer. Yet suffering by definition means we feel alone and desolate and far from God. Matthew and Mark record Jesus's cry of despair as the *only* words he says on the cross. I like that these gospellers refuse to paint a happy, clappy version of Jesus on the cross. Jesus knows personally what it is to *feel* forgotten, tossed aside by God.

The sixth word comes from John's gospel: *It is finished.* (John 19:30) John, who loves symbols and packs words and stories with multiple meanings, does so again here. Jesus is saying his life is finished, over, but also so is his work, his ministry, his purpose. We sometimes say "he's finished" to mean someone's hopes are dashed, his career is over, the relationship's severed. But we also say something is finished when it is complete, accomplished, whole.

In the seventh word, *Father, into your hands I commend my spirit,* Jesus exhibits control rather than crisis. (Luke 23:46) He says these words right after Luke records that the curtain in the temple is torn in two— this is the curtain that separated the people from the Holy of Holies, God's residence in the temple. Luke, who also told the story of the prodigal son and the lost sheep, indicates that nothing stands between us and God anymore, nothing can separate us from God.

Experiencing Good Friday during the pandemic, when the church was closed and empty, was both odd and fitting. Holy Week during a pandemic is like the seven words of Jesus meets George Carlin's seven words you can't say on TV. Not only did we feel separated from one another, but it seemed like God was self-isolating too.

Yet it allowed me to dive into Holy Week a little deeper. Good Friday is a day of great tragedy and death. Other dark days also stand out in history, after which nothing was ever the same. Pivotal days experienced by generations alive today include Pearl Harbor, Kennedy and King's assassinations, and September 11. The pandemic doesn't have a date attached to it, but the spring of 2020, the year the doors of the church were closed on Easter Sunday, will long be remembered and perhaps mark a time of change, when nothing would ever be the same.

We all have personal Good Fridays. The day we received a diagnosis, the day we lost a loved one, the day of a divorce or breakup, a day our hearts or dreams were crushed. The original Good Friday by itself is anything but good, but we know what happens three short days later. Our personal Good Fridays are rarely redeemed in three days. More like three years. Or thirty.

The day of Jesus's death can be called good only in light of the resurrection. Good Friday acknowledges that awful, horrible, painful things happen, and we might think that God has forsaken us. But Good Friday, like our own Good Fridays, is pointed toward resurrection.

Seeing the divine in each other will keep us caring and connected. Drawing from the divine within ourselves will give us courage to serve the human and hurting parts of one another, as well as to trust that the third day, the resurrection, is indeed within our sights.

Pericope (2019)

I watch enough British television and movies to note that the cure to every kind of cold or trouble begins with the words "Let me put the kettle on."

Such reassuring words mean someone wants to take the time to take care of you. Soon you will be offered a seat and a warm cup to wrap your hands around. Someone will sit across from you, and in the time it takes to sip your tea, someone will listen.

I have never experienced clinical depression. I have other brain malfunctions, most of which cause me to be less sensitive to people who suffer differently from me, and completely incapable of understanding spreadsheets and how bonds work.

I depend upon others in numerous ways. Paul says that is how "God has arranged" us to be. He likens the community of faith to be like one body, so we "may have the same care for one another. If one member suffers, all suffer together with it; if one member is honored, all rejoice with it." (1 Corinthians 12:24-26)

The pursuit of wellness is different for each of us, but if we are to reach any measure of health, it cannot be done alone. Individual wellness is always a group project. Maybe that's why wellness starts with "we," and illness with "I."

Most healing begins with someone who says to us, "Let me put the kettle on."

CHAPTER 24

HOLY WEEK: HOLY SATURDAY

I FEEL COMFORTABLE in a cemetery. It is like browsing in a library. A hush falls. Countless stories surround me. Epitaphs, like book titles, intrigue me, and I try to read between the lines.

There are two places in Old Jerusalem that claim to be the site of the cemetery where Jesus's body was buried. Scientific and historical evidence aside, I prefer the site called the Garden Tomb.

The noise and frenetic pace of Jerusalem dissolves upon entering the Garden. Though situated next to a bus station, the Garden immediately comforts and quiets the soul.

The tomb is a cave and spacious enough to walk inside. The stone that covers the door to the tomb is not as I had imagined. Instead of a large, bulky boulder, the stone is round and flat, like an oversized coin. As was the practice in the first century, the stone sits inside a narrow track. Similar to the way a sliding glass door works, the stone can be rolled within the track to block the tomb's doorway or to give access. Seeing this gave a new visual in my mind to the women's question on Easter morning, "Who will roll away the stone for us from the entrance to the tomb?" (Mark 16:3)

I have officiated and preached at hundreds of funerals and burials. The Reverend Marty Hedgpeth coached me on the liturgy—how to read the moment and the prayerbook's rubrics. There is a tendency to make what the deceased did in life overshadow what God does in death, or as Emmy Terrell advised me for her funeral, "don't allow the eulogy to render me unrecognizable."

Funerals can be occasions of shared joy and gratitude. My father's funeral was a day I treasured because of who came, what was said and how much my father's spirit thrummed among us. Funerals can speak to deep questions and wonderings about how God works or doesn't work in the world. For instance, I don't believe God chooses our time of death. I don't believe God decides who has cancer, diabetes or dementia. I don't believe God elects to save some from a fire, accident or battle, but not others. Yes, we are in God's hands, but to love anything or anyone involves relinquishing control.

Dorothy Sayers, in her play, *The Devil to Pay*, suggests that God sets aside power for something more precious than control.

> ...*Something* there is, perhaps,
> *That power destroys in passing, something supreme,*
> *To whose great value in the eyes of God*
> *That cross, that thorn and those five wounds bear witness.*[38]

That "something" could be our freedom to shake our tiny fist at the heavens, if we so desire. I have a feeling "something" is what gives our life meaning, and also, what makes our life meaningful to others.

Death, stony and unyielding, cannot be rolled away. Death is stuck, hogtied, immoveable. But hope and courage and love cannot be bound or shut down. They find a way. They rise up out of every tomb.

Of the countless soloists I have heard at funerals, one stands out above them all. Jim Whiteside stood in front of a packed church at the funeral of his twenty-six-year-old son, Bill. Though his heart was broken, there was a song left in it. Jim sang one stanza of *Abraham, Martin and John*, first sung by Dion in 1968.[39] Jim's version went like this:

---

38   *The Devil to Pay*, by Dorothy Sayers, page 72, published in 1939.
39   *Abraham, Martin and John*, written by Richard Holler, 1968.

Has anyone seen my son, Bill? Can anybody tell me where he's gone?
He loved a lot of people, but it seems the good die young.
I just looked around and he's gone.

Jim didn't sing loudly or even particularly well. Bill's death was immoveable, but the current of his father's love never stopped.

The church has no music or liturgy for Holy Saturday and remains as silent as the tomb.

Sometimes silence is all we receive from God as well. The time between disaster and relief, disease and healing, death and life can be excruciatingly quiet and quiescent. We do not know exactly what happened in the tomb, but believe that somehow, some way, God was doing for Jesus what God has been doing since the beginning: closing the gap between us.

Four months into his presidency, James Garfield, an unusually popular president, was shot by a mentally ill man. The year was 1881, and the correlation between hygiene and health was not widely accepted. Garfield's doctors didn't believe the recent European scientific theory of "invisible germs," and placed their bare hands into Garfield's wound. Garfield suffered terribly as a massive infection, caused by his doctors' ignorance, slowly killed him. Meanwhile the country, still polarized and divided twenty years after the Civil War began, became united in concern, waiting on pins and needles for news of their beloved president's health.

After two summer months of agony in Washington's oppressive heat, Garfield asked to be taken to the seashore, and doctors thought it might help him. A seaside home in Elberon, New Jersey was offered for the President to use. But how to get him there when any movement caused him great pain?

The Army Corps of engineers devised a suspended water bed for Garfield to lie on, so he would not be jostled against anything hard.

The Pennsylvania Railroad offered to transport him the two hundred fifty-mile trek and suspended other rail travel to speed his arrival. But the railroad track stopped one mile from the seaside cottage. Moving Garfield into a wagon for the last mile would have been tortuous for him. The people of Elberon came together to build the last mile of railroad track in *one night*.

First the road had to be leveled and graded, and carts of rubble cleared away before any track could be laid. As workers toiled into the night, the Elberon Hotel sent sandwiches, and volunteers poured gallons of lemonade for the sweating laborers. Older children held flaming torches to provide light for the workers.

The track was built in time, and Garfield's train pulled up to the cottage.

Almost.

The train could not climb a slight incline at the end of the makeshift track. Undeterred, the townspeople got behind the train and *pushed* it the last few yards to the door. Garfield spent the last two weeks of his life greeting the sunrise at the cottage in Elberon.[40]

Holy Saturday embraces every devastating silence from God that leaves us feeling forgotten, rejected, even spurned. Easter is the proclamation that God's generosity and ingenuity is always laying a track to reach us, to bring us from loss, despair, brokenness, failure to newness of life.

---

40   I first learned this page of history in *Destiny of the Republic: A Tale of Madness, Medicine and the Murder of a President* by Candice Millard, copyright 2011.

Pericope 2021

We have a key to our house hidden outside, and its "secret" location has not changed in over a decade. My children's friends all know where it is. Service providers to my house know. The three strangers who picked up our dog when she escaped from our backyard—they know. I figure people who rescue a lost dog are not the sort to rob us.

Doors are important. They are even spiritual in nature, for of all the things in this world that Jesus could have chosen, he said "*I am the door.*" (John 10:7)

Over the centuries the church paid a lot of attention to doors, relishing the role of determining who is in and who is out, who is welcome, who is not. You would think Jesus had said *I am the wall*, and not *I am the door.*

Churches have inflicted much pain and endorsed horrific theology by slamming doors to the poor, to women, to the enslaved, to the divorced, to the mentally ill, to gay, lesbian and transgender people, to anyone who questions tradition or authority, or anyone who is fortunate enough to find spiritual renewal, truth and comfort in other religions or practices different from what the church offers.

The key to Jesus's door is not hidden but where he has always told us it would be. Jesus proclaims that the way of loving and giving, the way of sacrifice and service, the way of forgiveness and mercy, is the door, the gate, to abundant life.

Anyone can enter because anyone can love, anyone can be merciful and kind, anyone can be generous, anyone can serve.

We stand at a threshold in the pandemic. We are like those awaiting a birth or a death, or the time between a job interview, an audition, taking a test and learning the outcome. We are in flight, having taken off from one place and not yet landed wherever we are headed.

Could it be that in this time of isolating we are not only being saved *from* something, but also being saved *for* something?

Something wonderful. Something healing. Something deeper. Something better. Something that will open doors in our hearts and minds we didn't know we had.

Chapter 25

Easter

A teacher shared with me her student's definition of Easter. The second-grader wrote: *This is why we have Easter because Jesus rose from the grave and if he sees his shadow he has to go back.*

The Easter story can be a difficult story to understand, and it's made even more complicated if it somehow gets mixed up with other holidays. A story that includes an execution, betrayal, a graveyard, and a dead person made alive again can be particularly challenging to explain to children and even to adults. But the bottom line is this: Christ's death has somehow made us right with God and given us the grace to always start fresh—even after failure, loss, humiliation, and death itself. How Christ's death accomplishes this is the stuff of many different theories and theological formulas. But no explanation is ever adequate to the reality.

Easter tells us the ending of every story. The empty tomb and the resurrected Christ proclaim that no matter our failures, no matter our mistakes, our pain, our loss or suffering, no matter how far afield we stray, no matter how mean, selfish, or deceitful we are, there is nothing outside of God's power to transform, redeem, give life, and make new. Easter says that life comes from the tomb. Easter is that happy surprise, the astonishing gift, the undeserved chance to start over. Easter is the sunlight splitting our darkness; it is forgiveness setting us free. Easter is a longed-for healing, the birth of something beautiful and new and compelling, the presence of peace when life is falling apart, the possibility of comfort when we are suffering, the promise of new life in the face of death.

This is not to say that the life that emerges from every death justifies that loss. Easter does not sugarcoat suffering or death—remember, Jesus emerges from the tomb with the marks of the nails in his hands. But in every situation, we do not have to settle; we can make space to see, as Richard Rohr writes, what God's love can make of it.[41]

A parishioner told me she was taking her teenage son on a trip to Europe, along with her son's stepmother. On purpose. That is what God's love can make of it.

I watched a story on the national news about two people who lived fewer than one hundred miles from me.[42] Collin Smith, of Asheboro, North Carolina, was fourteen and played three sports—football, basketball, and baseball—when he was in a terrible car accident just before his freshman year of high school in 2005. He was paralyzed from the chest down, unable to walk and with limited use of his arms and hands.

Collin and his family are members of a church in Asheboro, and a man named Ernest Greene is also a member of that church. Ernest heard about Collin's accident and paralysis, and he felt that God was calling him to help Collin. He did not know Collin. Ernest was a retired man in his sixties and said he did not have anything else to do. He knew that Collin's parents both worked and could not afford the care Collin would need. He approached the family and volunteered to help.

For the next four years Ernest arrived at Collin's house early and got him up, literally picking him up, dressing him, and driving him to high school and back home again at the end of the day. The high school provided Collin with an aide who pushed his wheelchair from class to class and took notes for him. When Collin graduated, Ernest knew that the only way Collin was going to go to college was if he helped even more.

---

41   *Radical Grace: Daily Meditations* by Richard Rohr, page 150, copyright 1995.
42   *Paralyzed Graduate Credits Retiree with Helping Him 'Pick up the Pieces'* by Josh Elliot, ABC News, June 6, 2013.

For another four years, Collin attended High Point University, and Ernest was with him the whole time. Ernest would get up early so he could arrive at Collin's house by six to get ready for the school day. Ernest drove Collin the forty minutes to the university, attended every lecture, took notes and wrote down what Collin told him to on tests. He pushed Collin's chair two to three miles a day from class to class. And when Collin got an internship to help with the High Point basketball team, Ernest stayed with him. Some days Ernest didn't get back home again until midnight, only to do it all over again the next day.

Ernest admits there were days he wondered what he had gotten himself into. He hoped to give renewed life to Collin, but he found he received it too. When Collin graduated from High Point, Ernest pushed him across the stage to receive his diploma, and then the president of the university surprised Ernest with an honorary diploma to the ovation of the students and their families.

God's love can make miracles through the Ernests of the world. But most of us aren't like Ernest.

The problem is we don't just want a happy ending for us. There is something dark and rank inside of us that believes that unless there are losers, there can be no winners. In *Hallelujah Anyway*, Anne Lamott mentions a cartoon in the *New Yorker*. One dog says to another dog, "It's not enough that we succeed. Cats also must fail." That is the human condition, Lamott writes.[43]

In order to feel like we have won, we must know that others have lost. We see this played out in the public arena, in politics, in businesses vying for the same customers, in divorce and small claims courts, even in classes graded on a curve. The cats must fail. We see it in scripture too. The prodigal son's older brother refuses to celebrate his younger brother's return. The workers in the vineyard who are paid a fair day's wage fume when other workers are paid the same for doing less work.

---

43   *Hallelujah Anyway* by Anne Lamott, page 9, copyright 2017.

Even some of the disciples try to negotiate for advanced status and a corner office.

Yet one of Easter's clearest revelations is that losers win too. Jesus is humiliated, rejected, abandoned, condemned, crucified—it's hard to be a bigger loser in Jerusalem than a man hanging on a cross.

When I was in Jerusalem, I walked what is called the Via Dolorosa or the Way of Pain. It is a famous path that pilgrims have traced for centuries. It is thought to be the path where Jesus carried the cross from his sentencing to his execution. I expected that walking that path would be a solemn, soulful experience, but Old Jerusalem is bustling with shops, tourists, and locals all going about their business. The group I was with stopped at each of the stations along the Via Dolorosa to read scripture and say a prayer. We tried to summon a holy experience, but it was like trying to have a worship experience at the mall the week before Christmas.

Then it hit me. When Jesus walked the same path, people didn't line the street with respect, crying and despairing the tragedy of his impending death along the way. No one cared! He was a loser walking down the street. People went about their business, paying him no attention. There was nothing that looked holy about his experience either.

Wow.

Easter celebrates the generosity and ingenuity of God. Even losing can lead to winning. And the word for that is *resurrection*. Sometimes we make wise and good choices and display kindness and compassion for others. But resurrection is about when you don't or can't or won't. Resurrection is God making use of our mistakes, even use of evil, and making use of death itself, to carry us over to fullness of life.

The season of spring with creation abloom and coming back to life seems like a perfect time to celebrate Easter. But after hosting a student from Chile, I was reminded that for half the world, Easter occurs in the fall, as blossoms wilt and brown, with the menacing cold and barrenness of winter approaching. How odd that would seem to us, and yet how powerful to proclaim God's capacity to make new, to give life, to restore relationship, to defeat death and all that threatens to diminish us, at a time of year when the days grow shorter and colder and darker. It would be like declaring life in the belly of a tomb, like being forgiven for our greatest shame and failure, like having hope return to our hearts after we had given up, like knowing death cannot separate us from those we love, like discovering that losing can be the path to greater love and meaning.

PERICOPE 2016

The 1972 Olympics starring Mark Spitz and Olga Korbut was the first I vividly remember. It felt like everyone read the same inspiring bedtime story and then talked about it the next day together. Perfect strangers had something to share.

Too often tragedy and horror fill our shared stories. During the Olympics, we shake our heads in disbelief of what beauty humanity is capable of instead of brutality. We cheer on athletes, and when they win, we feel like we win too.

Comedian Jerry Seinfeld does a bit where he talks about the problem with silver medals:

> "You win the gold, you feel good. You win the bronze, you think, at least I got something. But you win the silver, that's like congratulations, you almost won. Of all the losers, you came in first of that group. You're the number one loser."

Our culture places high value on winning. Yet our faith is centered around a victim. Jesus's death reeks of failure and loss. He is the number one loser … who somehow is winning. It is in his powerlessness and not his brawn that we find hope. For what unites us all is our imperfection. None of us wins all the time. Michael Phelps did not win a single medal in his first Olympics.

The good news of the gospel is that life is not a single-elimination game. It is our littleness, our brokenness, our familiarity with last place that opens us to receive God's mercy and grace. When St. Paul begged that his thorn be removed, he heard God tell him, "My grace is enough for you, because power is made perfect in weakness." Paul concluded that in stressful situations, "for the sake of Christ, when I'm weak, then I'm strong." (2 Corinthians 12:9,12)

Every Olympian has a story of sacrifice, dedication, and remarkable achievement. Every disciple does too, and the reward is not a medal but the realization that you don't need one.

CHAPTER 26

SCARS

IN 1874, MARY Cord was sixty years old and working as a cook in Elmira, New York. Her employer's brother was Samuel Clemens, aka Mark Twain. Cord's cheerfulness prompted Clemens to ask if she had ever known any troubles in her life. Cord responded, "Is you in 'arnest?"

Born a slave in Virginia, Cord married and had seven children. In 1852, her family was ripped apart when her husband and each of her children were sold. Cord lost touch with all of them but never forgot every little inch of them. The youngest, Henry, bore scars on his wrist and forehead from a fall. Years later, during the Civil War, Cord was living in New Bern, North Carolina, when black troops fighting for the Union occupied her owner's plantation and asked her to fix them breakfast.

Clemens' story was published in *The Atlantic Monthly* and he titled it, "A True Story Repeated Word for Word as I Heard It."

> I was a-stoopin' down by de stove, an' I'd jist got de pan o' hot biscuits in my han' an' was 'bout to raise up, when I see a black face come aroun' under mine, an' de eyes a-lookin' up into mine, an' I jist stopped *right dah*, an' never budged! Jist gazed, an' gazed, an' de pan begin to tremble, an' all of a sudden I *knowed*! De pan drop' on de flo' an' I grab his lef' han' an' shove back his sleeve, an' den I goes for his forehead an' push de hair back so, an' "Boy!" I says, "if you ain't my Henry, what is you doin' wid dis welt on yo' wris' an' dat sk-yar on yo' forehead? De Lord God ob heaven be praise', I got my own ag'in!"
>
> Oh, no, Misto Clemens, *I* hadn't had no trouble. An' no *joy*.[44]

---

44   "A True Story, Repeated Word for Word as I Heard It" by Mark Twain, published in *The Atlantic Monthly* in 1874.

Trouble and joy can leave behind scars. After Jesus's death, Thomas is famous for saying he will not believe reports of the resurrection until he shoves back Jesus's sleeve and sees the nail marks in Jesus's hands. He wants to put his finger in the hole where the spear plunged into Jesus's side. History rags on Thomas for doubting, and forgets to give him credit for being the first disciple to put the pieces together. Jesus is more than a rabbi and mentor. Thomas proclaims Jesus to be "my Lord and my God." (John 20:28) But before Thomas's declaration, Jesus says "Peace" to the disciples, to his so-called friends who abandoned him in his hour of greatest need. (John 20:19)

The gospel records Jesus popping in and out of locked doors and conversations for forty days after the resurrection. That's a long time and the dozen stories we have likely only skim the surface. As one might expect, an encounter with a previously dead person freaks folks out. Some do not recognize Jesus, and then they do and rejoicing begins. Jesus is different and the same.

I hope to be different and the same. Less of this, more of that, but still me. I am comforted by the idea that my previously dead self will be different and the same.

On the Sunday after Easter, the gospel reading in church is not different and always the same. We read the story of Thomas meeting the resurrected Christ. As an associate minister I am frequently assigned to preach on the Sunday after Easter, commonly called "Low Sunday," because church attendance drops drastically after being packed the week before. After thirty years, I can't squeeze another sermon out of scarred-up Jesus walking through locked doors.

In my line of work, I see nearly as many scars as a doctor. When church member Lynette died, I checked the filing cabinet where the church stores parishioner funeral plans. Not everyone is thoughtful enough to write down their wishes and turn them into the church. Lynette did. In addition to her funeral plans, I was surprised to find two letters in her file. Nice personal stationary. She wrote her son's name on one envelope and her daughter's on the other. I was touched. Lynette gave herself the opportunity to speak from the grave, to reach out to her grieving children, to offer her last words to them.

I was impressed by her forethought. I could not wait to deliver her letters. What a tender surprise it would be. What a fabulous idea I will tell others to consider including in their file.

Lynette's children accepted the letters with a tremble in their breath and hands.

She wrote them each one sentence. Her final request: Don't let your father attend the funeral. Lynette didn't want her ex-husband dancing on her grave. Lynette might have died, but her scars did not.

My younger sister, Ginny, was nearly scarred by a car accident. Ginny and I, seventeen and twenty-one, jumped in our father's car to run a quick errand at the grocery store. Our father loved cars. He even enjoyed haggling at the dealership for the price. Once he bought a car, he started thinking about the next one. In what my mother termed his midlife crisis, Dad bought his first sports car—a white Mazda RX-7. He let his daughters drive it too. At my suggestion, Ginny took a shortcut crossing four lanes of traffic. We didn't make it all the way across. We were not hurt. Dad's car was. Spun one hundred and eighty degrees, it sat facing traffic the wrong way. Its crunched hatchback was open and askew like a broken wing. Glass littered the road. When he arrived at the scene, Dad fumed and muttered and threw his hands up in the air.

A wrecker towed the car away, and it proved to be fixable. Ginny was distraught, however, and vowed never to drive again. On the day Dad brought the repaired car home, he walked in the house, tossed the keys to Ginny, and said, "Get back on the horse."

Ginny and I bear no external scars from the accident. The internal wounds healed in a way that increased our love for our father, and made it more likely for us to forgive and trust and love others. In one post-resurrection story, Jesus gives Peter the keys to the kingdom. I think Peter, who denied Jesus three times, might have felt like Ginny did when Dad handed over his keys.

Jesus's scars and Thomas's doubts are both important for us to see. We fear that our brokenness and screw-ups, our questions and hesitancies, disappoint and insult God. Like a losing English soccer team, we will get relegated. Dropped down a division where the victories are lackluster and trophies tarnished.

The word *innocent* comes from the Latin for "unwounded." But we all show up guilty and lame at the pearly gates, our scars intact, our truth and consequences bared.

Doubts are human and helpful. Doubts indicate that our brains are working. Doubt is not the opposite of faith. Unwavering certitude is. Faith puts its arms around doubt.

Wounds do not block growth or joy. Doubts are not signs of weakness or disrespect. Stop for a moment and consider what good news this is.

Sean and Heather Bonner's twenty-year-old son, Sean Jr.—dimple-faced, towering, charming, a college athlete—died by suicide at school. Sean and Heather's grief shellshocked them. Were there red flags that their son was suffering? In hindsight, they could see a few pale pink indications at best. They had hundreds of questions and agonized over what might have helped their boy.

They went to the college and wanted to speak with their son's suitemates. Surely his buddies could shed light on the tragedy. Did they notice how troubled he was? Did he say something to them?

Sean and Heather met first with their son's resident adviser, who barely knew their son, and his tears surprised them. They awakened out of their nightmare to see how many others suffered, and they did not want their son's death to cause more pain.

Sean and Heather realized Sean Jr.'s suitemates could be irrevocably harmed by what happened next. They were merely boys who needed compassion not questions. They needed to be comforted and embraced. Sean Jr.'s death was not their fault. His friends did not neglect him. As Sean bravely said at his son's funeral, the cause of Sean Jr.'s death was mental illness.

Sean shared their story in a small support group with others whose loved ones also died by suicide. My tears welled and the image of Jesus standing before Thomas took my hand.

Sean and Heather stood in their son's dorm surrounded by his friends, just as Jesus did in the upper room. Like Jesus, with their wounds unhidden, they breathed words of peace. In Sean and Heather, Jesus crossed through another locked door, their scars also sources of pain and peace. When the battered and broken minister to the anguish of others, I am deeply moved. I am newly converted to the way, the truth, and the life revealed to me by Jesus of Nazareth.

By the way he treated people, loved them, forgave them, respected and honored them, Jesus's life is a window for us to see what our lives our capable of becoming. His life is also a door, through which we are welcome to enter and live in the Kingdom of God not only after death, but as its citizens here and now. When we show up like Jesus did, our lives also become doorways for others to enter. Our lives preach, but only if the "p" is silent.

PERICOPE (2009)

Tim and I moved to Charlotte on a blazing hot July day. The air conditioner in our newly purchased home would not turn on. So on our first day as homeowners, we bought an air conditioner.

Our realtor recommended the name of a small company to help us. Norman, the company owner, took one look at me (seven months pregnant) and stayed at our house until 10:00 P.M. installing the air conditioner. Norman said he couldn't stand for us to have a bad impression of Charlotte on our first day in town. Norman sweated in the heat all day, determined to get us cool air before we went to bed that night.

My husband said what Norman did reminded him that he would rather see a sermon than hear one any day. I agreed that Norman had "preached" a very fine sermon to us that day.

When I wrote Norman a check, I asked the name of his company. "His Way Heating and Air," he said. With a little more conversation, I learned that Norman, a Seventh-Day Adventist Christian, named his company because he intended to run his business His way.

Through the years a pattern developed. We hired Master Painters to put a fresh coat on the house. We didn't realize the company was named for *the* Master. Big C Electric installed ceiling fans. Turned out the C stood for Christ. Fish Window Cleaners arrived with the Christian fish symbol on the van.

I think about Norman today because it's hot and my house is cool, but more so because he reminds me that being a disciple of Jesus Christ is not only about prayer and worship and reading the bible. It's also about living and working His way. If it's possible to install an air conditioner, paint a house, and wash windows His way over other ways, it's possible to do the laundry His way, take a deposition His way, call on a customer His way, mow the lawn His way, and greet our loved ones His way.

Of course, we'd all rather see a sermon than hear one. Even better, we can be a sermon.

Acknowledgments

I am not sure it is possible to write a book based on sermons that makes anyone interested to read it. I have given it my best shot. Thanks to all those who encouraged me to write this book, especially Chip Edens. Thanks to my mom who marked up my writing in school and taught me the importance of clarity and commas. Thanks to my dad who taught me that nothing teaches faster than a good story.

Thanks to my husband, Tim, who told me decades ago that no one complains about a sermon being too short. Thanks to my children, Caroline, Julia Gray and Rob, who provided wonderful fodder and have held up well as preacher's kids. Thanks to my grandson, Sam, (and all my future grands), whose smile melts my heart and makes me want to write a book while I still can.

Thanks to my editor, Geoff Smith, and designer, Steve Mead.

Through the years, I did a lousy job of recording the bibliographic information of stories or excerpts from books I incorporated into my sermons. I did not put footnotes (with page numbers, copyright, article titles, etc) in my sermons which were heard, not read. For the most part, I was able to provide that information for this book, but there are instances when I was unable to remember or locate my sources, and those instances are noted.

Thanks to the congregations where I have preached over the span of my ministry:

> St. John's Episcopal, Broad Creek in Fort Washington, Maryland, where I preached my first sermon and cut my teeth on parish ministry;
>
> Emmanuel Episcopal in Alexandria, Virginia where I was ordained to the diaconate;

St. Philip's Episcopal in Coral Gables, Florida, where I was ordained to the priesthood and became the first woman parish priest in the state of Florida; and

Christ Episcopal in Charlotte, North Carolina, where I arrived pregnant with my first child and serve today as a grandmother.

Thanks for listening and making me believe God had something to say to you through me.

Made in the USA
Monee, IL
05 November 2021